Praise for *Choosing ME before WE*

"Christine Arylo has written a wise and inspired guide on how to become the woman you'd need to be in order to attract and draw in the extraordinary love you've been looking for."

— Katherine Woodward Thomas, author of
Calling in "The One"

"*Choosing ME before WE* empowers women of all ages everywhere to connect within, fall in love with YOU, and let your romantic relationships be yummy side dishes to the most important entrée — your relationship with yourself. A savory, sassy read for every woman seeking more than a fleeting fairy tale."

— Kimberly Wilson, author of *Hip Tranquil Chick*

"Christine Arylo advocates for every woman to have the love she truly craves and deserves. Reading *Choosing ME before WE* will empower and challenge you in ways that are both nurturing and effective. Starting with her own personal experience, Christine offers the tips and tools a woman needs to fall in love with her ultimate soul mate: herself. And from that foundation, she can find a 'he' and create a healthy and supportive 'we.' Every woman should have *Choosing ME before WE* on her nightstand."

— Christine Hassler, author of *20 Something Manifesto*

D0047846

CHOOSING
ME *before* WE

Every Woman's Guide to Life and Love

CHRISTINE ARYLO

New World Library
Novato, California

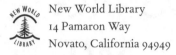

New World Library
14 Pamaron Way
Novato, California 94949

Copyright © 2009 by Christine Arylo

All rights reserved. This book may not be reproduced in whole or in part, stored in a retrieval system, or transmitted in any form or by any means — electronic, mechanical, or other — without written permission from the publisher, except by a reviewer, who may quote brief passages in a review.

Text design by Tona Pearce Myers

Library of Congress Cataloging-in-Publication Data
Arylo, Christine.
Choosing ME before WE : every woman's guide to life and love / Christine Arylo.
    p.   cm.
Includes bibliographical references (p. 206).
ISBN 978-1-57731-641-1 (pbk. : alk. paper)
1. Self-realization in women. 2. Self-perception in women. 3. Self-acceptance in women. 4. Women—Psychology. I. Title.
HQ1206.A79 2009
155.6'33—dc22   2008044940

First printing, February 2009
ISBN 978-1-57731-641-1
Printed in the Canada on 100% postconsumer-waste recycled paper

New World Library is a proud member of the Green Press Initiative.

20   19   18   17   16   15

To all women — past, present, and future —
who have dared to live from their heart and soul
and have had the courage to believe that anything is possible

Contents

Part One. ME

Part Two. HE

Part Three. WE

Acknowledgments

Choosing ME before WE is the result of my own personal journey of discovery to find and love the real ME, to freely and fully express *all* of ME. Every step I took was possible because of the love, inspiration, and guidance I received from people who shared their gifts and hearts with me. To these people I give my heart-filled gratitude.

To Anne Wagner, the match who sparked me to tell my story: I am forever grateful, for you saw the writer and inspirational catalyst in me when I wasn't yet able to.

To my troupe of angels — the healers, spiritual leaders, and teachers who changed my perspective on life and helped me heal my wounds, repair my wings, and learn to fly again: thank you for helping me find the real ME. I send a special dose of deep gratitude to Vic Turner, Paul Escriva, and Maureen Riley, my Chicago trio of healers, who were there to catch me when my life fell apart.

To my soul sisters, Anne, Colleen, Danielle, Debra, Michele, Catherine, and Tarja: you made this book possible because of all that you gave me and all that you saw in me.

To my grandmother Virginia Schneider, who loved and encouraged me even when she thought I had gone crazy in California: thank you for caring about my happiness and supporting me as I followed my dreams.

To my writing coach, Ricky Weisbroth, whose guidance, willingness to not hold back, and totally honest feedback catapulted me into my role as a writer: your influence will stay with me for the rest of my life.

I also thank all those who helped me make this book and my message, in all of its forms, physical realities. I offer an extra special thank-you to my editor, Georgia Hughes; my publicist, Kim Corbin; and the entire team at New World Library, whose insight and partnership ultimately made this dream possible; to Jan King at eWomen's Publishing Network, for your sage advice every step of the way; to Dava Guthmiller and Noise 13, for designing a book cover I love; to Lin Lancombe, Patricia Aburdene, and all the other women who read my first draft, for your honest feedback early on; to Paula Goldman, for your generosity and inclusiveness; to Rich Fettke, for your never-ending enthusiasm and guidance as my coach; to the San Francisco Girltalkers, for inspiring me with your stories, laughter, and wisdom; to Sherri Smith, for your fabu design work on my brand, Girltalk...taking it deeper; to Jay Kamins, for being the best web guy ever; to Laura and Lori Hardy-Thompson, for being top-notch legal eagles; and to Peggy Klaus and Bobbi Silten, for your heartfelt mentorship.

And thanks to all who supported me on my path to living and loving ME. You never asked me to dim my light; you only asked me to shine brighter! A big hug to Deborah Jones, Ariel Spilsbury, Pele Rouge (Grasshopper thanks you), all my Mountain Lions (meow), the Thought Leader Gathering community, my Nine Gates family, and of course my 13 Moon sisters.

Most of all, I thank Noah, my soul partner and best friend. Your support and love has been unwavering and unconditional from the day we met. Every step of the way, you have been my true partner. This book and the vision I set out to make a reality became possible because of what you gave and continue to give me. The gratitude I feel for having you in my life is inexpressible.

And lastly, to every man, woman, animal, and child who ever touched my soul, especially the four-legged jewel of my heart, Nanook: thank you for allowing me to experience the magic that is you, which ultimately is what inspires me to do what I do.

Let's Get to Know Each Other

*H*ave you ever felt that you walk the path of your life alone? That you are the only woman to ever make painful, stupid mistakes? To settle for less? To desperately desire love above all else? To yearn for a real partner so much that it hurts? Have you ever thought, "Why is every woman but me in a great relationship? Why can't I be that happy?" Or found yourself rejected by the person you love, and figured that something was wrong with you?

When the devastating breakdown of my fifteen-year relationship stabbed me, at the age of thirty, like a wild boar's tusk ripping through my heart, I was convinced that I was the only woman who had ever made such a complete mess of her life. I felt alone, rejected, and furious that I had deceived myself for so long. That I had given up my "self" to keep the love of another for years, only to be left with a heart torn to shreds. What I realized shortly after the initial blow of my relationship's end was that I had failed to understand that, above all else, I needed to honor the most important relationship in my life first — the one with myself.

This ending became a beginning for me, in which I learned many things. I finally got that I didn't need to feel so damn alone in my experiences — I had sisters on the crazy and confusing journey of being a woman. For better or for worse, as women we have many of the same stories, heartbreaks, obstacles, and expectations. I also learned that we don't have to remain captive to the limiting beliefs swirling in our psyches and in society, which keep us far from our dreams. We *always* have a choice. Along life's path, we all have the opportunity to gain wisdom from our mistakes, the self-awareness that comes from healing our wounds, and clarity by claiming our needs.

If we are lucky enough to wake up to the immense power we have to create our lives, we have a responsibility to share our stories and insights with others. Otherwise, the true power of our realizations is lost. Sharing allows us to see ourselves in the words of others, gain witnesses to our personal journey, and broaden the possibilities that lie before us. Through sharing, we as women can provide the emotional inspiration that others can use to eliminate the "shoulds," the "musts," and the "cannots" that bar their way to creating the kinds of lives and relationships they truly desire.

I, too, relied on the wisdom and support of many women, some of them total strangers, to progress through my own "long, dark night of the soul." By watching others and listening, I learned that to fully and wholeheartedly love another I first needed to fully and wholeheartedly embrace my "self." This realization was a major source of inspiration in my decision to share my knowledge and experiences with other women through *Choosing ME before WE*.

The following pages take us on a journey together. In them, I share the wisdom I gained on my personal path as I went from being a person I thought I knew and loved to being one I actually do know and love. I share with you stories from my own adventure as well as those of my dearest friends, all women trying to find sources of love and happiness but often looking in the wrong places. And, I ask you to take a careful look at the life you have created and honestly answer the question "Am I honoring the most important relationship in my life first — the one with myself?"

Before we go any further, since we are going to hang out for the next eight chapters or so, I would like to give you the opportunity to get to know me better. While you may already know my name, Christine Arylo (pronounced ah-rye-lo), what you don't know is that my last name doesn't belong to anyone but me. Not to the family I was born to, not to my husband . . . just to me. When I was a teenager, I felt as if I were walking around the planet with someone else's middle and last names. So, being the "rebel" that I fancied myself to be, at the age of eighteen I boldly declared that I was renouncing my middle name and going on a search for a new one that fit *me*. I had the grand illusion that I would find this perfect name while on some special quest — maybe on a journey to Africa or in a magical passage in an ancient text. While it didn't happen like I thought it would — there was no excursion to a foreign continent — fifteen years later I did find the name, or rather, the name found me. While running next door to borrow some sugar from my neighbor, I met a visiting eight-year-old boy, who said to me, "Hi, my name is Orilo." The sound of his name rang through every part of my soul, and I knew I had found a part of me that I had been missing. It was as if my entire body just shook and I had been given the key to a long-ago locked door. The irony of the experience was that all I wanted was a cup of sugar, and instead I got the name I had been searching for. I changed the spelling to "Arylo," started using it as my writing name, and, when I got married two years later, made it my legal last name. Finally I had a name that fit.

Of course, my relatives back in Chicago thought I had really "gone California," but I can assure you I was both sane and grounded. The experience of finding this name was an expression of my beginning to be and love myself completely — two things I had been unable to do my whole life. In retrospect, I can see how hungrily I wanted to be loved and accepted for ME, to be totally free to be all of Christine all the time, without apology. Today, I understand how *my* decisions, especially those concerning relationships, had prevented me from expressing and loving ME fully.

Being ME was never easy, and for most of us it isn't, especially during the awkward growing-up years. As a child and a teenager, I was a little gawkier than most, blessed with glasses at age five, braces at eleven, and a mother who dressed me like I was either fat or funny looking (I still can't decide). I was a late bloomer.

Outwardly, my family appeared "normal" — middle class, a nice house, a dog, a cat, siblings, Mom the Girl Scout leader, and Dad the softball coach. But as in most families, our dysfunctions silently did their damage — alcohol abuse (my father drank too much), repressed emotions (my mother was far too busy to feel anything), and too little physical affection (though my parents loved me, hugs were hard to come by). My parents were not ogres. I was not mistreated, and all my material needs were met. They did the best they could, but our relationships lacked depth and connection because my parents, *like most people walking on this planet*, carried their own burdens of unhealed wounds.

Like everyone, I had my own traumas, and mine were connected to the departure of the most prominent men in my life. The first to leave was my father. A few weeks before my fifteenth birthday, he was killed in a car accident. What seemed like an innocent parting for the evening turned into one of my most life-altering events.

On that wintry Midwestern night, when my mom was away

on business, my dad decided to go out. He came to my room to tell me his plans and said to have fun with my friends. Of course, being a teenager, I immediately thought, "Awesome, no third degree!" My dad drove off in our red Volkswagen Rabbit and I walked across the street to my best friend's house, where a boy I had a crush on was waiting to pick me up in his 1973 Oldsmobile Cutlass. Little did I know that this boy would ask me to be his girlfriend, beginning what would become a fifteen-year relationship. Little did I know that in the course of one night, one man would enter my life as another one left.

The next time I saw my father, he was laid flat in a casket, with his face covered by makeup and a high-collared shirt to hide his broken neck. He had died instantly on impact on an icy road the night we went our separate ways for the last time. His death was something I would not understand or mourn until the age of thirty, when the boy who drove the 1973 Cutlass called off our impending marriage two hours before our engagement party.

Looking back, the ending of our relationship should not have come as a surprise. This man had stepped right into the hole my father's death had created. Only an eighteen-year-old boy at the time, he made a promise to my dead father that no man should ever make: "I will always take care of her." With that vow, the dynamic for a new father-daughter relationship was cemented, dooming any hope for a healthy love affair. To me, at the age of fifteen, this promise seemed like true love, but by age thirty I realized it was a death sentence. We had created a relationship in which this man, who was not my father, felt the need to take care of me. When I no longer needed to be taken care of, he left. There was no reason for him to stay in the relationship. I will never forget his words: "Chris, you just don't need me *enough* anymore." He continued, "I don't love you anymore. I don't want to marry you anymore. And, oh by the way, I've been cheating on you for the past six months."

In the wake of his proclamation I reeled, heartbroken, experiencing the most intense, soul-gutting pain I have ever felt. It was as if my entire understanding of life had been decimated in an instant, shattering all of my life dreams. During the first few weeks, I hurt so much that I actually thought I might die. You know the feeling: as if your heart has been ripped out of your chest, leaving a hole so deep and dark that you don't even have words to describe the pain. For me, the alternating waves of severe suffering, complete emptiness, and fits of anxiety were the only things that let me remember I was still alive. Only months later would I realize that this man had actually given me the *greatest* gift ever: my freedom.

The truth was, I had been holding our relationship together with pieces of masking tape for more than a decade, continually adding more tape, trying to hide the flaws and lies from everyone, especially me. All he did was rip the tape off, exposing what lurked beneath the thick layers. And boy, did it hurt! At the time I blamed him for destroying our relationship and my life, but in reality it was I, not him, who caused my suffering. Sure, he could have been gentler — but honestly, the ending had to be that severe. I would never have left him. I would never have given up on our relationship. I zealously believed that, above all else, "we were meant to be together." It was destiny. Romantic at the time, I later came to understand that our relationship had covered up *my* pain.

Most of the time, the pain had been easy to hide. As a duo, we were great at racking up material accomplishments. We bought two houses and started a business. I progressed in my career and education. Cars, motorcycles, and all sorts of "cool stuff" filled our lives. The contract part of the relationship worked. As so many other women do, I thought my guy and I could make the parts that were broken better. I believed that love was enough to overcome anything. However, the truth was that I had been settling for less than I wanted for a long time. And if I could have been honest with myself and acknowledged the warning signs — fights, breakups, cheating — I would have been the one to leave. Although it still would have hurt, I would have saved myself a lot of shock, blame, and suffering.

Honestly telling our story now, I can say that, although we loved each other as best we could, our love was based on the holes we each had inside, dysfunctional wounds developed long before we ever met. We fought too much. We were in constant battle for control, and I continually rebelled against the rules he created. He tried to impose curfews on me. He forbade me to sit on our kitchen countertops, the ones I helped pay for! I can laugh now at the absurdity of his demands, but back then they caused serious warfare.

We were so different. I loved life and people. He liked complaining about both. I was outgoing, and he was depressed, a lot. We disagreed about everything from where to live to how to barbecue correctly. Our fights were rough. We knew each other's sore spots and wasted no opportunity to poke them deeply.

In order to stay with this man, I turned a deaf ear to my inner voice and bargained hard with myself. I gave up on my true desires, on what really mattered to me. I wanted to travel the world with my partner, but instead I took trips in the United States with friends. I wanted to live in the city, but gave in to his desire for a big house in the suburbs. I yearned to live in California, and had wanted to attend college there and then get a job with a fashion design company. Instead I convinced myself that something in Chicago would suffice.

Then there were the weeks and months we were broken up, which happened often. At those times, I was actually happy — which I conveniently forgot when we got back together. Being ME was so much easier when I was apart from him, whether I was alone or dating during our breaks. When I was with him, I couldn't get what I needed *in* the relationship, so I looked for it in other places — other guys, a village of friends, and lots of partying. In the end, this guy and I had created a relationship that wasn't good for either of us, and after it ended, I vowed to never again settle for less. So far, I haven't.

Sometimes, I think my story makes me sound like a lovesick puppy or some whacked-out girl with a bunch of problems who couldn't get her act together. But outside the relationship, my image was totally different. There was no trace of the insecure girl holding on to an inadequate relationship, too afraid to be alone and terrified to feel the secret pain she carried. My colleagues and schoolmates saw me as a confident, put-together woman who went after what she wanted and who could accomplish anything. I was a successful marketing executive moving quickly up the corporate ladder. A good student, I had graduated magna cum laude and had been accepted into one of the top graduate schools in the country. I had many friends; people liked being with me. That is who the world saw. And they were right: I was and still am that woman.

But I had also been wounded as a young girl. Both my father and mother had been emotionally unavailable for most of my life. I had suffered silently because of losing my father, whose death was only the first of three I would experience by the age of sixteen: I lost an uncle and a best friend within a year of my dad. Only a sophomore in high school, I had no tools to process my emotions and no adults to help me. These events caused big wounds that never fully healed; they only scabbed over. Only when my fifteen-year relationship ended did they begin to heal. As my illusions and false beliefs about my relationship and life fell apart, I could no longer hide, although I tried.

After the breakup, and after weeks of tirelessly trying to piece "us" back together, I surrendered. Worn out from crying, begging, and bargaining, I turned to an outside source for advice — a wise older woman. Within moments of sharing my story and listening to the insight she so bluntly (and lovingly) provided, something shifted. I realized that, although I had not been the one to end my engagement, I did have a choice. I could continue to wring my hands and heart over a man who clearly no longer wanted to be with me, or *I could reclaim my life*. I chose the latter.

Now I *could* tell you that, like Wonder Woman, I woke up the next morning and reclaimed my life, but then my story would be a fairy tale instead of the truth. The reality was that, although I accepted the wake-up call, I was still a broken bird with twisted wings and a sad, sad heart. There were days when I didn't want to get out of bed (and didn't) and spent hours crying over old photos and memories. There were nights when I drank too much. I leaned on my friends, calling morning, noon, and night, often sobbing and always confused. This new path wasn't clear. I felt like I was fumbling in the dark, grabbing for something to hold on to. All I knew — based on nothing more than a feeling deep inside of me — was that I had to keep moving forward. I couldn't go back.

During that time, I discovered within me the spirit of a survivor and a deep faith I had never known existed. I didn't have to run off to the mountains of Tibet to find it; I just had to keep taking the next step to heal and find ME. There was no other course to take but the one that went straight into the gaping holes, the painful and scary places inside me that I had avoided for much too long. So into myself I went, and I finally began to heal.

I didn't know anything about "healing" when I first began my journey. My understanding of healing related purely to the physical plane, to watching, for example, a broken arm mend or a scab disappear. I had no idea that our spirits and hearts needed healing too. Lacking instructions on how to release my inner pain, I did something out of character for me. I asked for help. And one by one, people — therapists, healers, spiritual communities, friends, and mystics — began to appear. They became my troupe of angels, helping me to remember that I, too, have wings. They supported me in mending those wings so I could once again fly. This troupe of angels guided me in seeing what *could* be instead of looking back. Their guidance never became a quick fix that I could use to conceal the holes inside my heart and soul, but instead served as the medicine I needed to heal them. Step by step, I released the layers of repression and sorrow that had kept me from soaring.

That's when life started to get interesting. Three months after I set out on my path to healing, not only was I finally learning how to love ME but, by "chance," I also met someone — the man who would become my most influential teacher, my best friend, and my husband. You can imagine that so soon after the most devastating event in my life I was not looking for — or ready to be in — a new relationship. I had sworn off men for at least a year!

But there he was, this 6 3″ bald and beautiful man named Noah who brought a smile to my face and warmth to my heart. I know now that our meeting was not a coincidence. He was what I had been asking for (begging for) in a partner years before my breakup. My mistake had been in trying to *make* my "ex-person" into something he was not. (I use the term *ex-person* instead of *ex-partner* because my former fiancé and I were never true partners.) In my heart I know that, after our relationship ended and I made the decision to choose ME first, the universe wasted no time in delivering the *partner* I actually desired.

Dating Noah was a big part of my healing journey. I learned what a healthy, loving relationship *could* be, as opposed to what I had been conditioned to believe from watching my friends, relatives, and the media. I experienced firsthand that a relationship could be fulfilling for each of us and still allow me to be all of me, all the time. For the first time in my life, I experienced unconditional love. I learned to let my heart open without the fear that it would be stomped on.

It sounds blissful, doesn't it? I am happy to say that the reality is as good as the story. Today I have a healthy, loving relationship with a man who is a partner in every sense of the word. Of course it's not perfect, but perfection is never an attainable goal. Relationships take practice, commitment, and a willingness to go deeper, together. Throughout our courtship, there were times when I thought our relationship wasn't going to work. There were times when I actually tried to *make* it not work because I couldn't accept all the love and happiness the partnership brought me. How screwed up is that? There were moments when I questioned Noah's commitment to continue growing and changing. Our relationship could easily have become a codependent mess in which I relied on him to heal the oozing wounds left by my breakup. Only with our mutual commitment to be aware of and to overcome our individual problems and shortcomings have we maintained a deep regard and respect for the other. In this relationship, I have never lost myself, only found more of what's already there.

Because of the tremendous, freeing experiences of my own journey of healing and discovery, sharing my stories and the wisdom I found became a driving force in my decision to write *Choosing ME before WE*. I have seen too many of the women I love settle for less because they didn't believe the kind of partner they wanted actually existed, or, sadly, they didn't learn to love themselves first. In reality, the possibility for true partnership and companionship exists only when we choose to believe that these things begin with our relationship to ME.

I learned from my own journey that, if we are honest with ourselves and approach life with courage and faith, we *can* have the relationships we desire. Seven years after I started down my road to healing, not only do I have the relationship to myself and my partner that I want, but I also stand in a life full of adventures and realities that I never even imagined before. I know what's possible . . . and it is my dream that every woman will imagine — and find — this same sense of limitless possibility for herself. We are the only ones who stand in our way. My hope is that, by sharing my stories and experiences, I can help you demolish the limitations standing on your path, so that you can claim the boundless possibilities waiting for you.

You're Invited!

I am so excited that you've landed here, at the start of our adventure together, one designed to take you on a journey into your self. This book and the adventure you are about to take will help you create healthier, more fulfilling relationships. But make no mistake, this book is all about you, because that is where each of your relationships starts. While you will be asked to contemplate questions about your relationships and partner, these pages are not a workbook to discuss with your significant other. They won't help you stay in a relationship whose time has passed. They won't even help you catch a man in ten easy steps. What this book can help you do is discover and embrace more of the true you, so that you can make choices about your relationships while keeping the most important partnership in your life at the top of your mind: the one with *yourself*. Although no other relationship should matter more, most of us women think and act otherwise.

From birth, we are taught to look outside ourselves for answers, validation, and connection. We are conditioned to think of others first — husbands, boyfriends, children, parents, work, and friends. We subconsciously learn to believe in fairy tales and spend our lives trying to re-create them. Primed to build the American dream of college, good job, marriage, kids, and retirement, we attempt to adhere to this formulaic, linear path. If one piece doesn't happen when it's "supposed to," if our biological clock is ticking and no man is by our side, or if we lose any one of the parts, we feel like failures. With the pressures of time and society on our backs, many of us stop at nothing to attain the missing piece, often settling for less than what we really desire.

If we want a life better than the cookie-cutter version that has left women unhappy for decades, we must be willing to strip away the illusions we've built and take responsibility for the circumstances we create. Herein lie both the invitation and the challenge of *Choosing ME before WE*: Know yourself. Be honest with yourself. Love yourself. Trust yourself. First. Then consider HE and WE, never settling for less than what your heart and soul desire. Let's go over that again:

> The invitation of *Choosing ME before WE*: Know yourself. Be honest with yourself. Love yourself. Trust yourself. First. Then consider HE and WE, never settling for less than what your heart and soul desire.

Our journey together offers the possibility of finding new insights, perspectives, and choices about yourself and the relationships you've created. However, it will be only as rewarding as you choose to make it. Your commitment and courage will determine how far you go. Let me tell you up front that this expedition isn't a stay at a posh, five-star hotel. It's a put-your-boots-on (they can be designer if you like) kind of adventure. There will be places that you find hard to access, difficult to get past, and a little scary. But there are also destinations full of life, love, and endless possibility, which will catapult you into places where you can and do claim the relationships and life you really desire by saying "Yes!" to yourself first.

Whether you are in a relationship right now or not is irrelevant. Whether married, in a long-term partnership, living with someone, dating, or single, every woman can benefit from exploring who she is and what she wants, separately from what she already has or thinks she wants in man. The only reason for not exploring is the fear of what you will find. And, let's face it, not liking what you see won't make it any less true. Love yourself enough to find clarity about what is real and essential for you.

I wrote this book from the viewpoint of a heterosexual woman in relationships with men. While I fully believe that *Choosing ME before WE* is a book for all women, at some point I had to choose a pronoun, and HE was the one I've always related to. Whatever your lifestyle choices and sexual orientation, if you are a woman who wants to explore, discover, and love more of herself, who's willing to release limiting and destructive beliefs, and who wants a life that reflects her truest most magnificent ME, then this is a journey worth taking. All that's required is an affirmative reply to the invitation to know, love, trust, and be honest with yourself, before considering HE and WE, never settling for less than what your heart and soul yearn for.

The Road to Discovery: A Few Supplies for the Journey

In preparation for the road ahead, and as your reliable and trustworthy guide, I want to ensure that you bring all the necessary equipment. Fortunately, a trip of this sort does not require a lot of packing — always a relief for those of us who tend to overpack, especially because, on this journey, we carry our own bags. I am going to ask you to bring five items, each essential to getting the most out of our time together.

- Attitude
- Truth
- Intuition
- Courage
- Desire

Attitude

What you receive from the following chapters will depend largely on your attitude. If you are open and receptive, this will be an expedition of discovery, with the possibility of gaining insight into the deepest, most vulnerable aspects of your own heart and soul. But, remain closed to new or different ideas, and you'll miss much of the potential experience. Sure, you may come across the occasional inspiration, but nothing of importance will stick. You can tell yourself either "I'm going to breeze through this book," or "I'm going to take the journey this book offers and challenge myself to go deeper into ME." Make your choice now: a nice walk in the park, or an adventure with the potential to shift your life?

Truth

Don't leave home without absolute Truth, not the kind that bends to fit your picture of reality, but real, honest-to-goodness Truth with a capital *T*. Simple as it may seem, self-honesty is extremely difficult. We avoid asking ourselves hard questions that demand truthful answers. Often we skew the answers to fit our need for comfort and security, avoiding our insecurities and pain.

However, this has to change if we want to create the lives we say we want. You can be sure that, as you answer the questions in the following pages, you'll uncover your own self-deception and will have to make a choice — truth or illusion. I recommend truth. Illusion only keeps us trapped, yearning for what we don't have, looking past our own needs and dreams and, sometimes, even our own health. What I have learned the hard way is that ignoring the truth doesn't make it go away. Neither does bending it, understating it, or embellishing it. Leave those bad habits at home. Do yourself the justice of being totally honest. This journey is one in which no one else can see you. Being anything less than 100 percent truthful hurts only you.

Intuition

Don't forget to pack Intuition — that inner voice, that feeling when you just "know," your sixth sense. Intuition is a warning device and possibility finder. "She" never lies and always wants the best for us. I like to refer to intuition as "she" because, when I listen to what mine has to say, she really is like a best friend. Her advice has only one person's interests at heart — mine!

Unfortunately, most of us would never consider personifying our intuition, because we are so far removed from it. It took me thirty-one years to discover what and who my intuition really was. The reality is that most of us are taught to ignore or downplay our intuition. Being rational, great. Going with a gut instinct, good. Leading with a feeling, don't say that out loud.

The good news is that a woman's intuition is strong and, even if we have ignored her or dressed her up as something else for most of our lives, she never leaves. We can always regain full access. Later, we will spend a whole chapter getting better acquainted with our intuition, learning to trust ourselves as the best guide in life we could ever have. But for now, if you know where to find your intuition, pack her up. If you're currently estranged or have never been formally introduced, just leave room in your suitcase. You will have plenty of chances to become more intimate along the way.

Courage

To receive the most from what follows, you must be willing to go into areas of your life that you know exist but that you might not want to examine. Maybe it's the past, the present, or the future, or perhaps all three. Think of these as caverns that hold your fears, insecurities, self-doubt, and self-hatred, your entire collection of destructive thoughts. Courage will give you the power to move through the darkness and into the possibility waiting at the end of the tunnel.

Through my own journey, I learned that courage is not the absence of fear; it is the willingness to step into one's own fear that is truly courageous. The objective is not to be fearless. It is to boldly acknowledge, meet, and transcend fear in order to claim what we truly desire. Every person on this planet has fear; we differ in how we react. Some people simply exist, paralyzed by fear, and others choose to face it — they choose to live. Nowhere on this expedition will you be asked to suppress the feeling of fear; rather, you will be encouraged to walk right into it.

Usually, just by taking the first step, we realize that our fears were much bigger in our minds than in reality. Remember *The Wizard of Oz*? Dorothy and her friends feared the Wizard until the curtain was pulled back and they realized he was just a man. *Having the courage to pull back the curtain that hides your own fears can be just as liberating!*

Fear is a natural emotion that we feel whenever our stability, sense of safety, or sense of being is threatened. As we continue to delve into the deeper aspects of "self," we recognize that we have a choice: we can move through or avoid the fear. The Cowardly Lion in *The Wizard of Oz* discovered his heart and happiness only after he found the courage to step through his own fears. Like the Cowardly Lion, with courage we can each move through the fears that keep us from our hearts' desires. You are the only person who can claim the life you crave.

Desire

Make sure you pack the desire to know yourself better and love yourself more. If the goal of getting married, finding a new man, or changing your current guy for the better is your only purpose in taking this journey, don't bother stepping out the door. Focusing on that which lives outside of you will not bring happiness. Make the choice right now to make ME the most important person on this voyage. During the hard moments, when your truth and courage waver, when logic threatens to override your intuition, your unabashed desire to choose ME will ensure that you do not settle for less than your heart, mind, and spirit desire.

ME Reflections and Delving Deeper

Throughout the next eight chapters, I will ask you to reflect on and think more deeply about your own life and ponder how the ideas discussed in this book can help you create the life and relationships you really desire. Only by making the perspectives and wisdom that I offer your own can you really change anything. For this reason, I suggest that, along with the items listed above, you also pack one or more tangible items: a journal and pen, a sketchpad and markers, your computer — some way to capture the insights you find.

"ME Reflections" are inquiries, interspersed throughout the chapters, that provide you with opportunities to further consider how the discussion pertains to you and your life. The "Delving Deeper" sections help you to take all you've learned in the chapter and apply it directly to your life. This gives you time to deepen your self-awareness and uncover new insights about yourself. "Delving Deeper" may include a list of questions to contemplate, a visualization to embark on, or a personal vow to take. Having used these inquiries and tools myself, and having shared them with friends and women I have met through my practice as a life coach, I can attest to their power to heal, yield insight and wisdom, give a sense of release, and so much more.

Think of them as doorways to new possibility, each with the potential for cultivating in you a deeper awareness about your life. Approach each question, visualization, or vow with anticipation and curiosity. Imagine stepping through a doorway with no idea about what's on the other side. What could be there? What is possible?

While there is nothing more important than connecting with ourselves, when was the last time you just sat still and took an honest look at yourself? Most of us are way past due. Lucky for you, this whole book is dedicated to helping you live and love you. Just remember, no matter what you uncover, don't retreat or hurry on to the next question or chapter. Stay and allow yourself the necessary time to uncover your truth.

If at any time these inquiries seem simple, check in with yourself and ask, "Am I actually taking a significant pause and being completely honest? Am I 'doing' the questions as if they were a task I must complete, instead of using them to find answers inside myself?" Warning sign: if it feels like "work," stop dead in your tracks. The goal of self-discovery is not labor or checking off a to-do list. You get no points for completing the questions. The questions here are not like those quizzes we all secretly love to take in women's magazines, where we cheat to fit into the category with the highest number of points. In this book, you'll find no right answers, no rankings, no one to compare yourself to — and no one else is listening.

And like everything else in this book, how you respond to the questions is really your choice. If all you want from a partner is a warm body that looks good on your arm, generates income, and provides a little fun, go ahead and treat these questions as a quiz. But if you're looking to create a relationship that lights you up, to find a mate who sees your soul, there is no other way than to know and love yourself first, and this requires intimacy with ME. Self-awareness demands going deep, with truth and courage, into yourself.

So, with your suitcase packed and your sturdy (but fashionable!) boots laced, get ready to plunge into your first adventure in "Delving Deeper."

Delving Deeper

- Why are you reading this book?
- What's really working in your life?
- What's not, and how would you like it to be different?
- Who is the most important person in your life today? If it's not yourself, why? Are you willing to make ME most important?
- What's going to get in the way of your completing this book? Time? Fear? Obligation? Something else? Can you leave it behind? Make a list of the things you need to say "yes" to and "no" to in order to finish the journey this book offers, and then make the commitment to participate in the whole adventure.

PART One

ME

CHAPTER  *One*

Knowing ME

Who Is This Woman Called ME?

GETTING BEYOND THE IMAGE
TO UNLEASH THE TRUE YOU

I cringe to think about the amount of time I have spent listening to women (and listening to myself) obsess over finding the right man or making the wrong man right. And for what result? Countless wasted hours spent on the phone and far too many glasses of wine consumed! Like a broken record, we complain about, analyze, and cry over men and our unmet desires for them to love us, to hold us, to marry us, and to do [fill in the blank] to us, with us, and for us. I myself have been guilty of starting far too many sentences with "If only he . . ."

This useless chatter among women has got to stop. No matter how many conversations, bottles of wine, or buckets of tears, the reality is that nothing ever *really* shifts when we point fingers at everything and everyone else. WE and HE *never* change until ME does. No matter how hard we try or how valiant the effort, we have absolutely no control over anyone but ourselves. The harder we try to manipulate, fix, or save our men and our relationships, the more exhausted and resigned we become, without ending up any better off.

Fortunately, there's another option available, and that is to really get to know ourselves. Not the images we present to the world, but the truest expression of ME. The quality of our relationships, and everything in life for that matter, starts with ME, not the other way around. We ultimately determine the HE and the WE by who we choose to be. It's as straightforward as an equation: one ME + one HE = two people creating one WE.

Our relationships are mirrors of ourselves. If we are emotionally, mentally, or spiritually unhealthy, our relationships become reflections of our wounds. Our partners reflect how we honestly feel about ourselves. If we don't respect and honor ME, neither will our partners. If we don't feel whole within ourselves, we will find a mate to fill in the holes for us — hello codependency!

I finally figured out this dynamic after recognizing the universal phenomenon called the Law of Attraction. In its simplest form, this law states, "Like attracts like." Translated to relationships, it means we attract people like us, men who reflect exactly how we feel about ourselves. Truly love yourself, and you can manifest a man who has the capacity to love unconditionally. Live as an unhappy victim of your circumstances, and along will come a mate to help you create that reality. If you are somewhere in between unwavering self-love and self-loathing victimization, it could go either way — good or bad. Yes, whether you like it or not, you are 100 percent responsible for the partner you attract and keep in your life. Only by changing your inner self can you alter your reality and relationship.

Law of Attraction: Like attracts like, so what kind of HE is your ME attracting?

What's Going On Inside YOU?

Let's face it. Not a person walking this earth is perfect. In fact, perfection is an unattainable and rather ridiculous goal. Imagine how much trouble we'd avoid if we could just surrender to our imperfection and let everyone else off the hook too, especially our mates. This would free us up to focus on the only part of the equation under our control — ME. All our relationships begin with ME . . . leaving us with three options:

OPTION 1:

> unhealthy ME + unhealthy HE = unhealthy WE

OPTION 2:

> healthy ME + unhealthy HE = *still* an unhealthy WE

OPTION 3:

> healthy ME + healthy HE = finally, a healthy WE

How "healthy" are you? And I'm not referring to your physical shape. Healthiness, in this context, isn't about a good heart rate, an impressive résumé, a stable financial portfolio, or doing the "right" things. It isn't about eating good foods, practicing yoga, or completing a few rounds of therapy. While all these things contribute to a healthier and more complete you, I'm talking about real, solid emotional, mental, and spiritual health, the kind that comes from a deep acceptance of and connection to your truest self. I'm speaking of the kind of sovereignty you carry in your core, always knowing that you are enough, with or without a man, exactly as you are right now. It is the deep belief inside your soul that you are whole and complete in and of yourself.

From this place of health and wholeness, we take 100 percent responsibility for our lives and everything in them, including our relationships. Awake to who we are, who we've been, and who we're becoming, we make conscious choices. We stop *reacting*, stop being unaware of and irresponsible about our own impact on our lives, and we start taking control of our existence. Only then can we stop settling for less and stop believing that "some" is better than none. Only then do we start creating the lives and relationships we want.

The length and path of your individual journey to health and wholeness will differ from that of every other woman, but make no mistake, everyone must make such a journey; no one gets a free pass. We all carry wounds. We all seek to more deeply know ourselves. We all must take an active role in our own emotional, mental, and spiritual health.

Being healthy and whole demands that at some point we do, at the very least, three things, in no particular order. One, we awaken to who we really are, separate from any outside influences, and embrace our truest selves — the best, the worst, and everything in between. This requires nothing short of brutally honest and compassionate self-awareness. Two, we commit to being and living our truest selves for the rest of our lives — self-awareness that sticks around forever. And three, we stand face-to-face with our fears and pain and heal them, making ourselves whole again.

Before self-awareness hit me smack in the face, thanks in large part to my shock at my fiancé's departure, I was blind to how unhealthy and "holey" I really was. My operating principle for life had always been "I'm fine. Everything's fine. No big problems here." If someone had asked me back then, "Are you healthy? Are you whole, in and of yourself?" honestly, I would have thought that person was a nutcase. I wasn't in the market for a shrink, and self-help lingo wasn't in my vocabulary. Working hard to keep my facade of a happy life and relationship intact, I labored to shove self-awareness away with the tactics I knew best: dismissal, sarcasm, and righteous self-confidence. I was, after all, "doing just fine."

Sure, I knew I had some unresolved issues, but I was oblivious to the depth of my grief and insecurity. How would I have known? I was "doing" my life really well — great job, big house, and the bling-bling ring. Of course there were signs — too much partying, an inability to be alone, and settling for a relationship that made me unhappy 80 percent of the time. But like so many women, I was a pro at creating a busy life that *appeared* successful, even to myself. It had me running so fast I didn't have time to question my happiness, let alone honestly *admit* I was seriously unhappy. And since most of my role models and friends were doing the same, there was no one screaming, "Hey you, stop!"

Getting a two-by-four to the heart two hours before her engagement party will surely change a woman's perspective on life, but I don't recommend it as a course of action. Being proactive — choosing to embrace self-awareness and accept 100 percent responsibility for your life before the universe delivers a wallop — is a much better choice. Making a truthful, no-nonsense appraisal of our selves, including our deepest fears, isn't easy, but the necessity of doing it is nonnegotiable if we're to create the lives and relationships our hearts and souls desire.

The remainder of this chapter is dedicated to helping you examine your own levels of self-awareness and wholeness. The rest of your journey, in fact the rest of your life, must start here. After all, everything starts and ends with ME.

♥ ME Reflections ♥

- Which unhealthy or healthy relationship equation (ME + HE = WE) do you find yourself in today or most often?
- What about ME creates that reality? In what ways are you healthy emotionally, mentally, and spiritually? In what ways are you unhealthy?
- What would you like to be different?
- What are you willing to do about it? What three actions can you take to become healthier?

Self-Awareness or Autopilot: It's Your Choice

Which has been your operating mode of choice? Are you self-aware — that is, are you centered in a deep sense of knowing who you are, do you understand why you do what you do, and do you take responsibility for the results? Or are you on autopilot — that is, are you asleep to your own motivations, anxieties, and limiting beliefs, and oblivious to the fact that your subconscious thoughts and fears are actually fueling your choices? Maybe you're living somewhere in between, sometimes making conscious decisions and, other times, mistakenly believing you're in control — even when you are, in fact, reacting to influences you're completely ignorant about. Chances are, unless you've made a conscious *choice* to be self-aware, you, like most people, operate mainly on autopilot.

One of the most common expressions of autopilot life is dating the same type of man over and over. Different name. Different face. Same baggage. We've all had that friend — or been that woman — who broke up with, even divorced, one man, only to find herself in bed with someone else who had the same basic flaws. Maybe guy 2.0 was better looking, made more money, and wasn't quite as big a jerk, but he still brought out her painfully familiar insecurities, fears, and defensive tactics. Perhaps she ended up slightly better off, but she was probably still miles away from her heart's desires. Too many women, including me, have attached their hearts and souls to men who weren't good for them, because, having blind spots, these women were too unaware of their mistakes to create anything different. Until, that is, they decided to change something inside themselves. Until they chose to take themselves off autopilot and honestly get to know themselves.

Since we actually have a choice in the matter, how is it that most of us not only choose autopilot but also fight hard to keep it driving the show? We embrace our limiting beliefs, fears, and suffering in lieu of jumping into the limitless possibilities that come from living our truest selves. We convince ourselves that it's perfectly logical and unequivocally safer to stay on autopilot, fiercely protecting our comfort and perceived security. Much easier to do this than deal with our real feelings. Much simpler to blame someone or something else than to look inside for the truth.

Think about it. How many unhappy people do you know who are painfully blind to the part they play in their own misery? While it's obvious to you what's going on, no matter how much advice you give, they just don't change, and their self-created mishaps keep on coming. And let's face it, we've all been there, clinging to a situation or relationship, unwilling to see the truth about ourselves and everyone else involved, unwilling to turn the switch from autopilot to awareness.

My autopilot phase lasted fifteen years — the length of my relationship to my now former fiancé (not a coincidence). Our blind spots fit each other like a glove, and together our unhealthy MEs created a very unhealthy relationship: unhealthy Christine + unhealthy HE = really unhealthy WE. For me, autopilot was a necessary tool of survival; it let me deny the many ways in which our relationship didn't work, which was the only way I could remain sane and stay connected to him. It enabled me to avoid what subconsciously drove me to stubbornly refuse to give up on the relationship: my own painful holes and the disturbing reality that I was unknowingly trying to re-create (and heal) my parents' dysfunctional relationship.

No wonder I fought so hard to stay on autopilot and in this unhealthy WE. The parallels to my parents' relationship were uncanny. Just like them, I had created a relationship consisting of two very separate people living in one house. Fixing my partner's problems of rage and depression became my version of my mother trying to get my father to stop drinking. My relationship, like theirs, was devoid of physical affection and laughter. And there I was, in a relationship of my own choosing, in which I was painfully lonely and craving love, just as my parents had been. What upset me most was not that I had re-created my parents' relationship but that I had been oblivious to its influence on my choices. I had been blind to my own motivations.

On autopilot, we have no idea who or what is really influencing our decisions and ultimately directing our lives, because most of our motivations and choices stem from subconscious influences. We base the majority of our decisions on ideas and beliefs we've learned from people who are, or were, not fully healthy and whole. Our choices are guided by the silent pressures of society, parents, relatives, and friends — until we decide to snap out of it and distinguish our own voices from theirs.

At some point on her personal journey, every woman must separate herself mentally, emotionally, spiritually, and sometimes even physically from these influences. As clichéd as it may sound, we must each find ourselves — our beliefs, our dreams, our unique imprint on the world. Only then can we make conscious choices about our lives, make decisions based on what feels right in our hearts and souls. Only then can we reap the benefits of self-awareness and responsibility.

❤ ME Reflections ❤
WHAT DO YOU CHOOSE?

- What has been your major operating mode: autopilot or self-awareness? Think about your relationships with partners, with friends, with family, and with your career.
- While growing up, what patterns or situations did you experience in your family, with friends, and in your community? How have these shown up in your relationships?

- What fears and limiting beliefs do you let drive your life? Think about a time when your fear stopped you from doing something you really wanted to do — for example, taking a new job, moving, joining a group, speaking up, or writing a book. What were you afraid of? What risk did you perceive? How real was that risk? How did your fear prevent you from living the life you really wanted?
- Think about the last three major decisions you made. What were your fears concerning these decisions? Write down the fears as if they had a voice and were speaking to you — for example, "You'll go broke if you try that" or "What if [insert fear] happens?" Where do these fears come from — parents, friends, society, previous experiences?
- Are you willing to make a *conscious* commitment today, right now, to choose self-awareness? If so, what changes must you make in yourself to honor that promise?

Know Your Holes; Heal Your Holes

The great thing about making a commitment to knowing your truest self and understanding your motivations and beliefs is that it opens up your ability to see the fears and painful wounds that you unknowingly allow to drive your life. Aware of the holes, you actually have the potential to heal and make yourself whole again. This all gets a little clearer with the following visualization. Take out your imagination here and visualize the following.

Imagine yourself standing in front of a big, round wheel of cheddar cheese, all smooth and orange. Say "hello" to the cheese. This cheese is you! Yes, I am asking you to think of yourself as a hunk of cheese — remember we're playing a game. Don't worry, you don't have to smell like cheese, just be smooth like a wheel of cheddar. This creamy but solid hunk of dairy product reflects you at birth — it's whole.

Now fast-forward through your life and notice that, as you age and have experiences, the cheese changes. Its color begins to fade from bright orange to pale yellow, and the unblemished surface becomes pocked with holes. Your smooth cheddar has transformed into a chunk of Swiss cheese, full of craters. These holes represent the wounds you received throughout life, times when your feelings were hurt, events that brought sadness or embarrassment, and moments you withstood any kind of physical or emotional pain. And we all have them! There's not a person alive who hasn't been "holed." The question is, what do *you* choose to do with yours? Some of us will heal our holes and become whole again, while others will continue on, year after year, living a holey, unhealthy existence.

Unfortunately, most of us decide to ignore our holes until the universe brings them screaming to our attention through some kind of life-altering event — a death, the loss of a job, a breakup, financial ruin, a health scare. There's a long list of techniques the universe uses to get our attention, making it impossible for us to ignore these gaping holes any longer. But that doesn't stop most of us from trying really hard to keep our holes hidden, since, after all, there are a million options at our disposal for what I call "hole stuffing."

What's your preferred hole-stuffing activity? Unhealthy relationships that divert your attention so you don't focus on ME? Hard addictions like alcohol, nicotine, or gambling? Soft addictions such as shopping, food, or television? Busy life and career, never stopping, pausing, or feeling? We all have them, whether we want to admit it or not. Having these diversions is nothing to be ashamed of. Heck, we are, after all, human beings with all kinds of lurking temptations that can prevent us from looking within for answers. However, just because your preferred hole-stuffing activity is available to you, this doesn't mean you have to activate it. What we each owe ourselves is a commitment to heal instead of stuff.

Before my wake-up call, I was what you might call a professional hole stuffer. My preferences for avoiding reality included a codependent relationship, alcohol, nicotine, and a busy, successful career that left me no time to really feel my emotions. All these stuffers were tremendously appealing, effective, and destructive. My ex-person, however, had functioned as the most effective stuffing for my holes, and when he got pulled out of some very deep wounds I had been avoiding, every single one of my wounds became exposed. Although I was oblivious to it at the time, I hadn't toiled so hard to make our relationship work because of my "undying love" for this man. It was because I needed him to fill my wounds. Letting him go meant facing the wrenching, emotional pain in my soul caused by big events like the death of my father and the murder of a best friend, as well as the quieter wounds, like my feeling of loneliness and fears of abandonment, which in the end were much deeper and more painful.

While I was with him, the thought of being without this guy was far more painful than experiencing a little unhappiness or some unfulfilled dreams, and I was willing to pay this price. In exchange for an unsatisfying relationship, I had a man by my side to help me feel safe, loved, and cared for, which I didn't know how to do on my own. Our relationship became a hole stuffer for the intense yearning I had for unconditional affection and love, which is ironic because I never received either from him.

Over the years, I've had to forgive myself for the times when I almost snapped out of autopilot but lacked the courage and will to follow through. There were times when I started to pull out the stuffing in my holes — during our numerous breakups, my initial investigation of Buddhism, my attempts to quit smoking, and my paltry two sessions of therapy. But I was never brave enough to go straight into my pain, to understand it and heal. Only after *he* left and I lay under the rubble of my life would I finally face my fears and wounds. So many of us get caught in this never-ending cycle, where we have moments of bravery and begin to step into the lives we really want, but then get scared and run back. We can't handle the pain of looking at the holes or the reality of ourselves, so we retreat to our unhealthy or unhappy situations that seem more bearable. Finally something happens, usually much more painful, that doesn't allow us to return.

One of the reasons I wrote this book was to give women an alternative to the two-by-four of suffering that comes when we avoid our truth for far too long. While pain may be mandatory in life, suffering is optional. If we can choose to address what scares us most, before something or someone else forces our hand, our pain actually becomes manageable, and transcending it becomes possible. I don't know about you, but personally, I'd rather avoid the deep despair of the pool of suffering altogether. And while it might not always be easy to choose not to suffer, we can at the very least choose to suffer for no more than minimal amounts of time. "Ow, that hurts. Let's stop that and move on" is a much better life strategy than "Ow, that hurts. Let me go in even deeper to feel some more pain."

It's certainly *understandable* why we work so hard to avoid truth — staying in relationships longer than is good for us; letting the fear of being without the men who are stuffed in our holes (and I am not talking about sex here) be greater than the pain caused by letting them go. But understanding this doesn't make accepting it okay. Every one of us owes it to herself to admit that she alone can heal herself, that no amount of love or support from someone else can make her whole. We must each recognize that stuffing instead of healing our holes creates a relationship that makes us depend on a man for love instead of depending on ME, the one person we can count on! This isn't to say that love from another is unnecessary, because every human being needs love. It simply has to come from ME first. We need to be mostly "hole free" to create a healthy relationship. After all, life is a journey of continuous healing. We must, however, honestly know ourselves and heal our biggest wounds before we can make healthy, conscious choices about HE or WE.

♥ ME Reflections ♥

- Think back through your life and answer two questions: What have been the really hard experiences? What's been painful about being ME — finding it hard to make friends, moving a lot, being a gawky kid, having busy parents, dealing with bullies, or any other experiences? Think back through each of your decades and write down the main "Ouch, that hurt" or "Wow, that was really hard" circumstance or event you experienced during each time period. Explain why it hurt or what was difficult. These don't have to be severe traumas, although they may be. Sometimes the less obvious ones cause the most suffering.

- Look over what you wrote. What have you healed? How have these experiences affected your life decisions and relationships? Which ones are still holes? What's the effect of not healing them?

- Think about your life overall. In what parts of it are you so busy doing things that you hide from what's true and avoid your feelings? How full of activities and focused on external achievements is your life? This includes everything from work to social time to surfing the Net to watching TV — anything but just being still with your thoughts and feelings. Do you ever just sit quietly, with eyes closed and no distractions, and notice your feelings, and then let yourself feel them completely? Why or why not?

- What emotions and feelings — from childhood or adult-hood — have you been suppressing? How do these hold you back from having what you want?
- Are you still resentful of or angry at anyone, including yourself? What holes has this caused? How would heal-ing the holes — by letting go and forgiving — make your life different?

Delving Deeper
DO I *REALLY* KNOW WHO I AM AND WHAT I WANT?

Until she can say "Yes!" to the question "Do I really know who I am and what I want?" with complete confidence and honesty, no woman has any business walking down the aisle or making other lifelong commitments. Unfortunately, many of us wish for the ring, push for a proposal, and even exchange vows before gaining a clear, grounded sense of who we are and what we want out of life. When we are little girls, dreams of princes, weddings, and marriage begin to enter our heads. As we mature into our teens and early twenties, these dreams become goals and, for some, obsessions. While mar-riage can be a wonderful, enriching experience, there is a critical step that comes before it, one that too often gets left out: learning to know, honor, love, and trust our *self* first and discovering the dreams we carry regardless of what another human being may want.

The path of self-discovery doesn't require celibacy or re-nouncing relationships with men. Actually, intimate bonds can help us grow and learn about ourselves in ways that being alone can-not. But life mates need not become husbands. We can be single, have boyfriends, lovers, and live-in partners, *and* go deeper into our bond with our self. Regardless of the path we choose or the men who come in and out of our lives along the way, we must spend time exploring life just for ME, becoming *self*-aware, healing our holes, uncovering our hopes, and discovering who we are under all the history, societal pressures, and expectations. Only then can we truly know the kind of life we want to create and the type of partner who will support and enhance that vision. By understanding ourselves, we become better equipped to recognize the partner who will be our best match.

While there is no predetermined age at which we know ourselves well enough to commit to a long-term partnership, in my experience, the magic number for most of us comes sometime after thirty — this was certainly true for me and my friends. Married, committed, or single, in our twenties most of us were still on autopilot, believing we had it all figured out. In reality we didn't have a clue. Looking back, I see that our teenage years through our midtwenties was a time for exploration and making mistakes without too much accountability (lawlessness aside). Trying hard to prove we were adults, we were still just kids when it came to self-awareness and healing our wounds. Somewhere around the age of twenty-seven, our eyes started to flutter open and notice that there was more to life than we had originally thought. But it wasn't until age thirty that most of us *started* to take full responsibility for all aspects of our lives. Although our awakening and healing process was finally under way, it took most of us at least a few years more to reach a solid level of intimacy with the core of who we were.

Think about your own life, whatever age you are today. How much better do you know yourself today than you did five years ago? The fact is, while we continue to discover more about ourselves for the rest of our lives, there are key periods of formation and self-discovery during which we simply have no business making lifelong commitments like marriage. I chose my first potential husband when I was fifteen! By the time I was thirty, when he proposed, my ideals for a man were much different. But there he was, and it seemed like we ought to get married. It was the next logical step.

So many of us succumb to societal and familial pressures to hurry up and get a career, find a guy, get married, have babies. When we have a boyfriend, the question is always, "When are you getting married?" When you get married, the question is, "When are you having babies?" It's a wonder that when we retire people don't ask, "So when are you going to die?" As a culture we are so fixated on where we are going that we can't just be good with where we are. And this really unhealthy tendency has caused too many women to rush into commitments way before they knew themselves.

Carli's Story

My dear friend Carli was one of those women who rushed into commitment. At the age of twenty-four, she married the man she had begun dating during her senior year of high school. After college, they moved to Chicago together but lived separately, until a year before Dave popped the question. For Carli, living together before marriage was a big deal, not because she cared, but because of what her parents would think. Young and unsure of herself, Carli felt that their opinion mattered greatly. So, when she and Dave started living together, the next logical step had to be marriage.

What may sound like a romantic proposal — vacation, beach, sunset — turned out to be one of the worst days of Carli's life. When her future husband, Dave, got down on his knee and took out a diamond ring, Carli now admits, what she wanted to say was, "No! I don't want to marry you." While she didn't know it at the time, it was her intuition screaming. She had no idea back then that she had intuition; she just knew that she felt tremendous pressure to marry this guy. It was the next step to take. But instead of voicing her doubts to anyone, even herself, she silenced her inner voice and let herself be driven by her fear of what people would think if she didn't marry the guy she'd dated for six years. Carli said, "Yes." A year later, they married. Six years later, they divorced.

I remember Carli, at the beginning of her engagement, as a bright young woman who was insecure and beautiful; smart and naive; driven and totally unaware of who she was. When I heard the news of her engagement, instead of offering the customary congratulations and "oohing" and "aahing" at her ring, I asked Carli about Carli because I cared about *her* happiness. Only twenty-seven myself and just starting to wake up, I wanted to know if marriage to Dave was what she *really* wanted. She said it was. I shared my viewpoint on getting married before the age of thirty and giving yourself time to know ME first. She said, "Dave and I are different from other couples. I am only twenty-four, but this is what I want." I didn't believe her, but I respected her decision. I attended her wedding, *and* I was the first person she told about her decision to divorce Dave, even before she told Dave.

A year or so before she turned thirty, Carli, who'd become a seasoned executive and was no longer naive or insecure, at least not professionally, could not continue to stay in her marriage. It didn't feed her passionate soul. She and Dave were living two different lives, and she was lonely for companionship. He loved to hang out at concerts in his Levi's and combat boots, and she liked to dine in spendy restaurants wearing her newest Gucci shoes. Her family took her and Dave on vacations to Spain; his family never left the town they grew up in. While Carli and Dave both liked to travel, and both had good careers in the same field, they fought like brother and sister, cutting each other down like fourteen-year-olds. There was no intimacy, friendship, or sexual connection in the marriage, and her spirit could not remain dormant any longer.

In the years following her divorce, after a lot of pain, recovery, and soul-searching, Carli began blossoming into a brilliant woman. She had always been successful in her career, but now she was coming out as a fully developed person, alive, free, and passionate about expressing her vibrant spirit. She had gotten out of the box that was her marriage. She was free to walk the path of self-discovery, to find the magic of who she was and share that with the world. The Carli of today — self-confident, self-aware, and on the road to health — would never have chosen Dave as her partner. He was the choice of a scared girl alone for the first time in a new city. But Carli had believed, at the ripe age of twenty-four, that she knew herself. Simply continuing to *date* Dave would have been a lot less painful.

Regardless of your age, the message is the same: Never make a life-long decision before you can say "Yes, I know myself. I am honest with myself. And I love her and trust her!" Challenge yourself to think beyond what society, your family, and your friends say is so. Don't blindly live your life according to what is "normal" or "acceptable," or make life decisions based on what appears to be the next logical step or simply because you don't want to disappoint someone. Far too many of us get caught in the trap of needing to be married, have kids, and buy a house by some magical age. Or think we are too old to start over. Give yourself a break. Focus on who you are and what you want to create in your life and go do that. To hell with what anyone else has to say!

So let's go even deeper into who you really are, today, and who you are becoming. The exploration of self is a forever adventure — we are perpetually growing and changing — but I've listed some of the questions you can ask yourself, *and answer*, while on the path to knowing your most authentic self. These questions are meant to be a starting place for your lifelong adventure of knowing, loving, and living you, inquiries that will help you know yourself and your motivations better. With a more intimate understanding of ME, you have so much more potential to create the life and relationships you really want.

Lights ME Up

- What five words describe you best? What five words describe you least?
- What is unique about you? What are your gifts and strengths? Think about the compliments you get from others, or what people often come to you for.
- What is most important to you? Remember times in your life when you were happiest. What did you have in your life — freedom, connection, truth, adventure, learning — that contributed to your happiness?
- What motivates you today? What would you like to motivate you? Notice the gap between the two. What is healthy and unhealthy about these motivations?
- In order to know yourself better, what are three things you can do?

Keeps ME Dark

- When have you been most afraid in your life? What was going on that made you afraid? What effects do those fearful experiences still have on you today?
- Which of your habits and choices are destructive? Think

about things that make you feel good in the moment but then leave you feeling bad afterward. Name three of your worst choices, current or past. Why did you make those choices, and what impact do they have on you today?

- What choices have you made to gain more security — have you stayed in relationships or jobs longer than you wanted to, chosen comfort over perceived risk, or become scared about money? What fears were these choices based on?
- How have you let your choices be influenced by societal or familial standards or expectations?
- What pressures do you put on yourself to be at some certain life stage by a specific age? When has this related to a healthy goal, and when has it been the result of an unhealthy attachment?
- How and when have you chosen comfort and safety over what you really wanted? What has this cost you? How has it affected your choices in relationships?
- What would you like to do differently?

CHAPTER Two

Truthfully ME

How Real Am I with Myself?

THE LIES WE TELL AND THE HONESTY WE NEED ABOUT OURSELVES, OUR GUYS, AND OUR RELATIONSHIPS

*L*et's face it. We have all lied to ourselves at one time or another because we couldn't deal with reality. In relationships, we've all clung longer than was good for us, turned a deaf ear to the sage advice of friends, and painted pictures about our guys that were fairy tales at best. Yes, like it or not, most women — and this includes you and me — are experts at building illusions and believing in their own lies. If necessary, we can and will *make* our lives appear to be what we *need* them to be, in order to hold on to our relationships, jobs, and material possessions and, ultimately, to prove to everyone, especially ourselves, that "I am happy."

This chapter's mission is, quite simply, Truth. It gives you an opportunity to get clear about just how real you are with you. How honest we *choose* — and it is a choice — to be with ME affects everything in our lives, especially when it comes to the HEs we attract and the WEs we create. And since we've boarded the truth wagon, let's be real and admit that being honest with one's self can be damn hard, especially in our relationships.

When it comes to HE and WE, it often seems easier (or at least more familiar) to live with lies, half-truths, and self-deceptions. We embellish our stories: "My husband is the best." "We are so happy." "Everything is great." We cling to romantic notions and socially acceptable, but totally unhealthy, norms; we ignore our intuitions and feelings when they don't align with our desired reality. It's absolutely understandable — but not acceptable — that we would engage in such self-destructive behavior. What woman wants to admit that her life is less than fulfilling? That she is unhappy in her relationship, to the point that she *wishes* she could leave? That she *needs* a man in order to feel comfortable and secure? That she knows it's time to end it but is too scared to be alone? That the guy she talked up to all her friends is really not all that? No woman I know! Nope, we take the seemingly easier route and avoid the truth for as long as possible. In the end, however, by ignoring what's real we do ourselves a great injustice.

In the pages that follow, you'll have the opportunity to use your relationships as a way to uncover how honest you really are with yourself. After a frank look at how our relationships often come from the illusions we create and the images we cling to, I'll expose five of the most common lies and their corresponding truths, ones I've seen in myself and the women around me. We won't leave this chapter until you've gotten clear about what your commitment to honesty with yourself really is.

Getting Real about Our Relationships

How many women do you think are totally truthful about themselves and their motives in relationships? Or about the HE they've attracted and the WE they've created? My experience says most of us are not. Unless we've consciously decided to do otherwise, we're firmly entrenched in the illusions needed to keep our relationships alive. And the worst part is, we *know* that we're lying to ourselves.

Sure, we're occasionally blind to our self-deception, but most of the time we actually know something is wrong. Yet instead of acknowledging it and facing it head-on, we usually work as hard as possible to cover up any uneasy feelings. While we're on autopilot, our natural reaction is to overlook and downplay our partner's behaviors, and the resulting events, that bother us. Even if we're self-aware, if we've failed to commit to uncompromising self-honesty we will lie about and make excuses for the men in our lives, and then, with the skill of a Hollywood actress, pretend that everything is okay.

Where does this get us? Exhausted, frustrated, and still unhappy is where! Eventually, no matter how hard our effort to keep the lies submerged, and how strong our desire to stay in our comfortable and secure ideal, deliverance comes, and it ain't pretty. Sometimes the things that we try to pretend aren't there — infidelity, emotional abuse, financial disaster, a loveless marriage — come crashing in, making it impossible to deny the truth any longer. Other times reality creeps in, taking the form of such things as disease or depression, often aging us well beyond our years. Regardless, truth always surfaces.

During my days as the queen of fantasy, I was a pro at making my life look good on the outside, convincing myself that I was happy on the inside. Of course, neither was true, but no one, not even I, could tell. It was what I now refer to as "living to fit the image." I took all the great skills I'd developed at my day job — marketing and building brands for well-known consumer products — and used them to incorporate myself into the image I had created of the woman known as Christine. I expended tremendous amounts of energy to keep this image intact, keeping as busy as possible, succeeding, socializing, and self-medicating — doing whatever was necessary to avoid facing reality. I became so practiced at avoiding my true feelings that it was second nature for me to believe in the ridiculous romantic notions I clung to and ignore the serious warning signs of an unhealthy relationship.

One of my favorite lies of all was "We were meant to be, so our love can conquer anything." Masked as a beautiful profession of love, this was nothing more than one of the many untruths I used to deny how dysfunctional my relationship was. It worked fabulously. It didn't matter that the love of my life just hurled a stapler at me, for example, missing my head by inches; he was only having a temper tantrum and it would pass. It didn't matter that this great guy spewed expletives at me almost daily; if I cried harder and tried harder, maybe he would finally love me. It didn't matter that there had been no sex in months; it would happen tomorrow. And it didn't matter that I'd had more dates with my best male friend than with him; our love was enough. I ignored the signs that my fiancé was cheating and convinced myself that we had a soulful, one-of-a-kind connection. Anything that jeopardized this picture was ignored or "reframed." Any threat to my comfort and security was locked out of my thoughts or manipulated so that everything in the relationship fit my twisted view. In my imaginary land, our bigger-than-life, all-encompassing love overshadowed the nasty actuality of my life.

Often, we mistakenly think that our illusions protect us, that they keep us from a truth that is much too scary. We so deeply want to believe our partner is *the* man we really do want, because our security and comfort depend on it. The thought of demanding change or leaving the relationship elicits such fear that we will do anything, including lying to ourselves, just to keep the illusion of serenity alive. So caught up in being afraid, we can't even spot our own self-deception.

It would feel fantastic to be able to say that I'm the only woman alive who ever created a fantasy world this elaborate, and it would be comforting to think that others have been spared the pain and embarrassment — no, self-hatred — I felt while coming to terms with my self-deception. But I know I'm not the only one. I know that a great many women have built their own fantasylands complete with their own sets of excuses.

For generations, women have been *surviving* their lives instead of nurturing the dreams and possibilities that might permit them to thrive. We stay in relationships that drag us down instead of lift us up. We play the victim, drowning in unhappiness, even though we're the ones who put ourselves underwater. We create grand illusions built on ideals of love and sacrifice, and we put ourselves last and the survival of our deceptions first, no matter the cost. Then, when our self-created brick wall crumbles, or our partner treats us with disrespect and unkindness, we get mad. We get infuriated at the people and circumstances around us, refusing to focus on the real perpetrators — ourselves.

The truth is, there is no one else to blame. We own our illusions and misery. The good news is, we also own choice. We can continue to believe our lies and build our illusions, or we can finally take responsibility.

❤ ME Reflections ❤

- What lies have you told yourself about ME, HE, or WE in order to keep a relationship alive?
- When have you bent the truth when telling others about your relationship or your guy? What are some of the specific fabrications you've told? When you examine these bent truths, ask yourself, "What was my real motivation?" Was it fear, the desire to fit in, the need to look good, or something else?

37

- What fears or truths that you almost faced scared you so much that you reverted back to illusions instead? Think about decisions you almost made but didn't follow through on. What was so scary that it made you run back to illusions instead? What did you run back to, and why did you believe that was safer?

Lies We Believe — and the Truths That Free Us

I can remember the first time it struck me that I was not the only one. At some level this saddened me greatly, but at another I felt relieved to know I wasn't the only woman on earth to tell herself lies like "He'll change for me" or "This time he really will be the man I want." Nope, as I sat among a group of women while listening to their stories one afternoon (an experience I have since had perhaps hundreds of times), I could almost feel my head nodding incessantly as other women shared their stories. "Uh huh . . . yes . . . exactly! I've done that too. I know exactly how you feel!"

While we are all fabulously unique women with different backgrounds, stories, and beliefs, we all fill our heads with the *same* lines of bull, and, surprisingly, despite our uniqueness, we all build identical illusions. What do we end up with? A heck of a lot in common. The good news is that this means we're in this crazy thing called life and relationships together. The bad news? If we are all walking around in the dark, believing in the same lies, how the heck are we ever going to find the Truth?

For starters, we can look at some of the most common lies we tell ourselves — statements women have professed silently or out loud, probably for centuries. Chances are, if you're female, then no matter your lifestyle, you've adopted at least one, and most likely more, of these lies. Beginning when we are little girls, and throughout our womanhood, the lies are reinforced by books, magazines, movies, television, parents, teachers, religion, and on and on.

What woman hasn't sat in a movie theater watching a romantic story and felt her own heart yearn for that special someone who could see her inner beauty, or held her breath at the thought that her love, too, could be the one to beat all odds? We've all believed that our relationships were special, that they were different from the ones around us that weren't working. If I were a betting girl, I'd wager that at one time or another most of us have tried to change a man. And, although efforts like this succeed all the time in the movies, let's face it, most of us don't have Hollywood screenwriters on our side.

We live in the real world, not in well-scripted stories. My challenge to you is to consider the following perspectives and find what's real for you within each lie and truth, and then be honest about how this has governed your choices and relationships. Ignorance is no longer an excuse.

1.
Lie: I can fix him. He'll change for me.
Truth: Only he can change himself, for himself.

How often does a woman marry thinking that she can fix her guy? Or delude herself into believing that she is *the* woman this man will change for, different from all other women who have previously tried? While I don't have the exact numbers on hand, I can tell you that the correct answer is: "Too many!"

This lie, that you can "fix" a man, is dangerous and destructive for at least three reasons and probably many more. First, appointing yourself as fixer is not only arrogant but a sure sign that you're avoiding something in your own life. Fixers love to focus on other people because it keeps the attention off their own problems. Second, no matter how special you are, you have no more power than any other woman to change this man. Believing anything else points to a severe case of self-delusion and unhealthy attachment. It's beyond arrogance. Third, since no one changes unless they want to (though you can be an influence), dedicating yourself to a cause like this leads nowhere but to suffering.

Let's look first at this fixing addiction women love to take on — transforming people, problems, relationships, anything that needs resolving, usually in the name of "helping." I was a self-appointed, professional fixer for fifteen long years. To me, "helping" my fiancé overcome his depression, to the detriment of my own health, was proof of how much I loved him. I believed that, because I could see beyond his struggle as a man to the little boy who desperately wanted love, I could be *the one* to make the difference. So I stayed, convinced that if I just kept trying or just loved him more, or differently, or without judgment or question, he would change — our relationship would improve, and so would my life. Fifteen years later, his problems remained, and so did mine. Trying to fix him — and the many other people in my life — had become an addiction. And like all addictions, it let me slide along on autopilot — a convenient distraction from looking in the mirror at myself.

Unfortunately, I am not the only woman with a predisposition for fixing men. How many times have you heard women say things like, "I know that in time, he will change. Once we are married, or once we live together, or once this or that or the other, he will be different." And then, how many times have you watched these women become stuck with the harsh reality of being connected to a man who hasn't moved an inch and probably never will? Or maybe you've been that woman yourself. In truth, changing the level of commitment in a relationship — marriage, kids, house — won't make any man really change. If he wasn't on the fast track to personal growth before, now that he has you, all motivation is gone!

How much a man does or doesn't love you is also irrelevant.

How well you do at trying harder, loving more, and doling out ultimatums is similarly immaterial. Don't waste your energy with thoughts like "If he loved me, he would change" or "I just need to be patient, be better for him, and then he'll come around." Get over yourself and realize that his unwillingness to change has nothing to do with you.

Which leads us to the second part of this perilous lie: What makes us think we have enough power over a man — what makes us think we're different from any other woman — that we can be *the* reason he changes? Women who love to date "bad boys," "Peter Pans" who will never grow up, or "confirmed bachelors" eat this lie up, believing unquestionably in their supernatural powers to make a man "good," grown-up, or otherwise ready for marriage. Without a doubt, a woman like this is convinced that he will turn "good" for her, that she will be the one woman he stays faithful to, stops doing [insert destructive behavior here] for, or finally settles down with. Unfortunately this doesn't usually happen. Even if the woman does get the ring and the husband, she won't get the guy she really wanted. It isn't that childish, bachelor boys can't grow up, but that they only become men when they choose to. No woman can make it happen for them.

Furthermore, why would you want a man to change for you instead of for himself? What would that say about the kind of guy he is? Think about it. Do you really want a man who is so uncentered and unconfident that he would alter himself for anyone else, including you? Doesn't having a man who knows who he is, who is willing to listen to new perspectives and then make his own decisions, sound better? Unless, of course, you're looking for a puppy dog to pull around on a leash. If you are, well, you're reading the wrong book. This book is about healthy relationships and healthy MEs, not about becoming a woman who can dominate or emasculate her man.

And one last point. We also like to fool ourselves with statements like "I love my current partner *more* than she did" or "He loves me more than her, so our relationship is different." This too is a big load of hairy bull. We don't love some people more and others less. Love doesn't work that way. It has been my experience that, as we become healthy and self-aware, we learn to love *better*, not more, to choose partners who have the *ability* to share their love more completely and clearly. By growing and healing, we learn to love from a place of wholeness instead of neediness. We realize that there is no imaginary reservoir of love from which some people get more and others less.

❤ ME Reflections ❤

Be honest about your own level of addiction to fixing others, your tendency toward unhealthy helping, and your destructive beliefs or attitudes about changing the guy in your life.

- When have you tried to change a man? How has it affected your relationships with yourself, your friends and family, and your career? The quality of your own life? How has it stopped you from getting what you really want?

- When have you lied to yourself about trying to fix a man, covering up your attempts by calling them something else, like "helping," "loving," or "saving him from himself"?

- Think about the types of things you tried to change in your partners. What is the common theme? What does this tell you about yourself?

- What is true today? Are you a fixer? Are you a recovered fixer or a fixer in recovery? How did you stop trying to fix men? Or how are you still trying to fix people?

- In what ways would you like to change your beliefs about fixing and your patterns of fixing?

If you have even a sliver of the I-can-fix-others lie lurking in your subconscious, I offer you the following set of promises that you can make to yourself, declarations that can help you transcend the destructive and arrogant patterns created by living with this illusion. They are the same promises I committed to after deciding to break my addiction to fixing, declaring retirement from the role of fixer forever.

SELF-PROMISE 1:

I focus only on changing ME.

SELF-PROMISE 2:

I will never try to change a man — ever. I may offer new perspectives or give my opinion if he asks for it, but I will refrain from actively attempting to make him someone he is not, even if I believe he could be better. As a matter of fact, *especially* if I think he could be better.

SELF-PROMISE 3:

I choose to be in relationships only with men who are honest, 100 percent responsible for themselves, and committed to being the best they can be — no exceptions.

The healthiest role we can play in a relationship is to be a partner, not a parent or a preacher. Yes, encourage your guy to be the best possible person he can be, but inspire him to grow and change by the choices you make for your own life. Don't push, prod, or drag any man along. You have better things to do than waste your time and energy on impossible endeavors.

2.
Lie: He's changing a little. He must be becoming the man I want him to be.
Truth: Minor modifications are not real changes. They are traps.

Throughout the course of a relationship, even the most non-evolved, sloth of a guy is likely to make minor modifications. Don't mistake these for real changes. They are short-term behavior blips and are usually provoked by things like fear, tragedy, and manipulation. Although the triggering event may shake a person out of his previous behavior pattern, these blips usually last for only a short time. Once the fear or grief subsides, or the person gets what he wanted, the old behaviors return. And we are left deflated, let down again, back at square one.

Here is how it almost always plays out. We get excited about the slightest degree of change in our guy, believing that the big one is just around the corner. We wait . . . and wait . . . and wait. In the best-case scenario, he stays at the same place the minor blip moved him to. In the worst situation, he reverts back to the way he was. Most likely, though, he lands somewhere in between. But regardless of where he lands, we are left to call again on our reserves of hope that one day this man will actually be the partner we want.

It's a roller coaster, and most of the time it leaves us absolutely exhausted or hopeless. We withstand this unpleasant ride by focusing on the highs, using the blips to sustain a relationship for years, conveniently forgetting how crappy we feel the majority of the time. Somewhere on this ride, a sign should be posted that says, "Beware! Blips can keep you tied into a relationship with the wrong person for a very long time. Do not wait around for temporary highs to turn into lasting change."

I continued to wait for real change for more than a decade, garnering no more than 10 degrees of shift when 180 degrees was required to make my guy the right partner for me. Sometimes a small behavior alteration would follow a big blowout between the two of us, the volcanic result of a million small events that built up over time. Family illness, our own health problems, or a friend in trouble were also great at catalyzing us to be on our best behavior; and then, like clockwork, when the difficulty passed, so did the good juju. It happened a zillion times over the course of our relationship — blips that never became real, lasting change. But, with the lie — that he was making progress — operating in my subconscious, I refused to see the truth: He was *never* going to become the right partner. Hell, he didn't even know what the word *partner* meant.

Becoming someone other than who we are today requires transformation, and a real shift of this kind demands brutal honesty with one's self, coupled with a willingness to let go of unhealthy beliefs, values, and attachments. Think about the changes you've made in yourself. How easy were they? What motivation finally made them stick? It probably wasn't another person. Even if you experienced a life-changing event, *you* chose to make and keep those changes; otherwise you slid backward into old patterns. Changing ourselves demands choice and commitment, no exceptions.

Consistent, truthful self-awareness and personal growth are hard work, which is why many people opt out of pursuing them — staying the same is just fine for them. And this may be okay for you too — being with a guy who will be the same as he is today for the rest of his life. For most of us, though, it's not enough, even if we lie to ourselves and say it is. If you're going to personally evolve, then you need to be with a mate who does so as well, even if not in the same way or at the same rate. A guy who sits around on the couch of life, content with his status as couch potato, won't be the right partner for you, no matter how much you love each other.

Be truthful with yourself about the man you choose. If he's not enough for you today, then chances are, he won't be tomorrow. While he doesn't have to be perfect, and you certainly don't have to like everything about him, you must be honest with yourself about what's negotiable and what's not.

People are who they are unless *they* make the decision to

CHOOSING ME before WE

change. This means that picking a partner based on his potential, believing that with your "help" he will become the man he can potentially be, is a bad idea. Yes, all men have the ability to transform, but don't treat your life like a slot machine. The odds are not in your favor.

❤ ME Reflections ❤

- How have you avoided the reality of your current or previous partner? Think about times you let yourself believe he was something other than who he really was, or that you fell in love with his potential. What were the results? What was your motivation?
- When have you settled for the blips? What happened during the blips? What were the common themes — when they happened, what he said, what you were experiencing in your own life? What were the lies you told yourself about the blips and your partner?

3.
Lie: We were meant to be together. He is the only one for me.
         [Insert any other romantic notion here.] This is "true love."
Truth: Professions of undying romantic notions do not equal love.

Oh, what a number the greeting cards, romantic movies, and so on have done on us! Sentiments such as "I'll love you forever," "You are my one and only," and "We were meant to be" fill our big screens, small screens, romantic novels, and sweetheart holidays, and therefore our psyches, subconsciously convincing us that "true love" is all about promises of "forever" and declarations of "only you."

The movies tell us that grandiose romantic gestures equal love.

What woman hasn't wiped the tears from her face while watching a movie, yearning to hear these words from her own man? Or watched another couple deeply enveloped in affection for one another and wished she had that kind of relationship? I sure have, and more than once.

Romance itself can be a wonderful part of a relationship. We all want to be seen and loved by our partners. Of course we want to hear "I love you" and be told how special we are, and there's nothing wrong with that. The problem arises when we use romantic ideals to avoid the truth.

Sometimes we let intermittent romantic gestures be the fuel that keeps us going in a relationship for years. After all, the greeting card holidays tell us that someone else's words written on cards signed by our guy once or twice a year equal love. I've sure been guilty of pushing the dismal reality of my relationship aside because my guy professed his "true feelings" on Valentine's Day, an anniversary, or some other special occasion. Yes, although we might have grown beyond blatantly chasing the fairy tale of Prince Charming, most of us long so much to be seen and loved by our guys that, when romantic gestures or proclamations come our way, we develop sudden amnesia about the real state of our relationships.

Sometimes our relationships are packed full of romantic declarations. Our relationships feed off these tidal waves of emotion, and we develop a *need* to hear these professions of undying love to fill our own deep "holes." What we really should be doing is asking ourselves questions like: What's missing inside of me that I need a man to tell me that his love is *forever?* Why can't it be enough that he loves me today? After all, he can't really promise more. Why do I need to know that I am the only woman my guy has ever loved so deeply? Isn't it enough to know that he loves me now for who I am? And, what makes me think that there is a scale for measuring the "trueness" of love, that lets me compare this love to any other love I've had? Who sets the standards, and who decides what passes for "real love?"

If you really think about it, the notion of categorizing love is ridiculous. However, we do compare degrees of love all the time, convincing ourselves that our past relationships weren't true love, or that our current relationship most certainly is. What the heck are we talking about? Love cannot be measured or compared, and in any case, nothing good ever comes from comparison. The real question is not, "Is this true love?" Love can't be anything other than true. The wise questions are: "Is this relationship what I want and what I need? Is it healthy, and am I healthy in it?"

The fact is, healthy relationships don't need professions like "I love you forever" and "You are my one and only." In healthy relationships — which are based on trust, respect, and intimacy — two people deeply connect and really see each other for who they are in the present moment. When intimacy is at the heart of a relationship, romantic gestures or words are about the present. They don't focus on comparisons to the past or make promises for the future. They never ooze because of codependent hole-stuffing; the energy exchange is clean and liberating.

Let's pause and bring this to life with a short visualization that will help you feel the difference between an intimate interdependent and a codependent connection. If you've never done a visualization before, no worries. It doesn't require any special skill, just a willingness to close your eyes for a few minutes. Think of this as a movie, one that plays on an imaginary screen in your head, your own private movie theater. If you're familiar with visualizations and have a different technique that allows you to see the moving picture in your mind's eye, then use it if you prefer.

Exercise: A VISUALIZATION ABOUT CONNECTION

Close your eyes and take a few moments to become still. Take a couple deep breaths and erase whatever is already on the screen in your head. Imagine a warmish silver rain washing down your body from head to toe, clearing all images or fuzz from your mind, leaving your mind's screen blank, as if on standby.

Once your mind is clear, envision yourself sitting by a fire with your lover, sharing a bottle of chilled bubbly or wine or sipping steaming cups of cocoa. Maybe some soft music is playing in the background. He looks adoringly at you and says, "You are my only love. I will love you forever. You are my everything. I need you so much, I would die without you." How does that feel? Expansive or suffocating? Heavy or light? Do his words make you feel like a person with your own identity, or do you feel wrapped (trapped!) in someone else? Did he just lay a grand piano–sized expectation on you?

Now erase the screen and let's start over. New movie. You and your partner are at the same fire, sipping drinks. All warm and cozy. Your partner looks lovingly at you and says, "I am so grateful that you're in my life. I love you so much for who you are, and I especially appreciate how you help me be an even better me." How does that make you feel? Relaxed? Warm inside? Are you expanding or contracting? Feeling larger or smaller? What do you notice about you and about him in this moment?

Let's take a moment for a movie review. The first scenario is a glimpse into a relationship based on need, attachment, and self-definition by association with another person.

Together, these form the solid foundation of something to avoid like the plague: the codependent relationship. In messy, unhealthy relationships, both people are guilty of hole stuffing, both are masking their own issues by focusing on the other person. Fed with unnecessary proclamations like "true love" and "forever," we often mistake these intertwined and twisted messes for romance.

The second scenario depicts an interdependent, healthy relationship, in which both partners know they are whole without the other. Separate and connected, they don't *need* each other to survive. Instead they *choose* to be together because the relationship allows ME, HE, and WE to flourish. This is the kind of relationship we want.

The traditional love proclamations used to sound romantic to me; I used them *all* the time in my previous relationship. And they may still sound romantic to you. But be honest about how the first scenario made you feel as you visualized it. It made me feel suffocated, as if someone were sucking me into him, trying to gain his security from me rather than letting me shine as ME. If you've been in this kind of codependent relationship, welcome to the club! I've yet to meet a woman who hasn't at least dipped her toe into one. It's just part of being human. As infants, we look to our parents for love and security — we are dependent. We need these things from them, and, depending on our luck, some of us get lots of love and security (among a host of other things), and some of us don't. Most of us fall somewhere in between. But no matter what we received from our caregivers while we were children, every one of us has to go through the individual journey of becoming an adult. This means growing into a wholly realized individual who finds love and security inside herself first, before she seeks love from a man or any other outside source.

My mantra? Keep the romance and the love. Get rid of anything that smells even slightly of codependency.

❤ ME Reflections ❤

- What romantic promises and declarations have you used most often? Say them aloud. What feelings, images, or thoughts do they stir up in you?
- What was your motivation for using these romantic declarations? What were you looking for? What need inside of you were you trying to feed? How have the romantic notions helped you to avoid truth?
- When have you let intermittent romantic declarations keep you satisfied in the short term? Why? What was the long-term effect? How did they contribute to an unhealthy relationship?
- What healthy expressions of romance and love do you want in your relationships? What's the biggest change you can make inside yourself to create that reality?

4.
Lie: He completes me.
Truth: Only you can complete yourself.

"He completes me" is one of the scariest statements I have ever heard come out of a woman's mouth! Seriously, it actually makes me cringe to hear a woman say these words — words that give away her power, self-respect, and self-worth. Believing and uttering this

CHOOSING ME before WE

statement is damaging to the very life of one's spirit, yet many of us believe it's one of the biggest compliments we can bestow on a partner. Either oblivious or in denial, we avoid the truth that "he completes me" translates to "I need a man! I need someone to take care of me and make me whole. I cannot be happy alone." A woman who makes such a claim believes, consciously or not, that, without a man to complete her, she is inadequate, that she is not enough, that what she offers the world and herself falls short.

I once believed this lie myself. I even felt envious as other women, from friends to actresses on the screen, proclaimed their "love" through the statement "He completes me." I can remember thinking to myself, "Wow, how great for her. She and her guy must really be in love. I wish I had that." My investment in this particular fantasy was substantial. And because I didn't understand how insidiously it had penetrated my belief system, I was blind to its effect on my decisions. I was totally unconscious of how it kept me paralyzed, unable to leave my ex-person for good. Whenever I tried to separate from him, I felt agonizing pain, as if part of me were missing. And it was. Whenever we broke up, the holes in me were brutally exposed, and I mistook the emptiness I felt deep in my chest for missing him. But the truth is, he wasn't missing; I was. I had failed to heal my own wounds with love and forgiveness. It was my wounds that were really causing the intense pain in my chest. I didn't get this until our final breakup, when I started on the road to making myself whole again, to trading in the lie for the reality of "I complete ME!"

Logically, the thought that a man can complete us is absurd, but since when does rational thought apply to love? So let's see what happens if we just go mental for a moment. If you believe a man actually completes you, what happens if he leaves, voluntarily or involuntarily? Do you become only half a person, or three-quarters of a soul? I certainly hope not! It would be rather hard to live life without this "completer" if you were only 75 percent you. Say your guy never leaves and you grow old together. The fact is, living with this lie means living the majority of your life believing that you are not enough, that you need someone else to make you complete. That is utterly sad. You deserve more — we all do. The totality of each person's unique spirit is magnificent. To never find yours would be such a loss.

It's important to understand that "complete" is not the same as "enhance." Finding a partner who enhances our life is wonderful, even essential. Meeting a man who has qualities we want to develop in ourselves can be a tremendous part of our personal discovery. Companion, teacher, lover — these are healthy roles for our mate to play. Need fulfiller, hole plugger, completer — does anything about these roles sound inviting or healthy?

My ex-person played the role of hole plugger, and together we created a codependent mess in which we needed each other to carry each other's pain. Today, I am married to a man who helped me become a better ME. I have grown more quickly and deeply because of his unwavering encouragement and friendship. By watching him, I learned to slow down, laugh more, and be more compassionate. When my ex-person called off the engagement and left, I capsized. My life fell apart because I used him to complete ME. If Noah — my husband — and I were to separate, of course I would be unspeakably saddened, and my life would be diminished without his presence. But I would still be a whole and complete person. Together, we create a much stronger bond because we both come to the relationship as whole people.

In case you feel skeptical about what I've said, let me be clear: We are not engaged in a semantic expedition. The words "he completes me" have intention. The words we use matter! Feel the energy that goes into "he completes me" and compare it to "we are stronger together." The first statement limits, the second opens.

"Completes me" takes one person's energy and pushes it into the places in the other person that are empty. "Stronger together" is expansive. The energy in the relationship builds because it's not being spent on filling the other person's holes.

♥ ME Reflections ♥

- Play around with the words yourself. "He completes me." "I complete me." Say them out loud. Visualize them. How does each phrase make you feel?
- When have you believed that a man completed you? Why did you want to believe this, and what did it give you? What choices did you make because of this belief?
- How would your experience of that relationship be different if instead you believed that you completed you? What would be different about how you felt about yourself?

5.

Lie: He loves me more than "her," and one day he will pick me. One day we will be together.

Truth: He's never leaving her, and could you trust him if he did? And oh yeah, what about your self-respect? And by the way, what did "she" ever do to you to deserve this?

Whether you've been the "other woman" or been her friend, you've probably seen this scenario played out in real life, and — oh, what a surprise — it's a reality wholly different from what we see in the movies and on television. This lie is all about deluding ourselves into believing that we are better than the wife or the girlfriend, convincing ourselves that, if the guy ever did choose us (which seldom happens), he would be different (he never is). Instead, the sad reality we're left with is usually loneliness, bitterness toward a woman we don't even know, and a lifetime of waiting around and reacting to whatever the guy chooses to do. He's available to see me? Great, I'll be available to him. He can't see me? I'll make other plans. 99.9 percent of the time, his needs will come before ours, until we get really mad, have a fight, get our needs met for at least the time being, and end up continuing the same unhealthy relationship.

How is it that smart, seemingly together women make such a self-destructive, painful mistake? Why is it we are always asking, "When are you going to leave her?" or telling ourselves that "he will leave her soon," instead of asking the real questions: "Why am I engaged in a competition with a woman I don't even know? Why aren't we both demanding a faithful partner? Where is my self-respect?"

While we can roll excuses off our tongues with ease to justify our behavior, the reason we keep hurting ourselves is anything but simple. I've been watching one of the most beautiful, big-hearted, career-driven women I know put her life on hold for five years for a guy she says is "the one." The problem is, he's always had a girl-friend — the same girlfriend — which is shorthand for "He's not dumping her anytime soon." This other woman is the one he brings home to his parents on holidays, the one he takes to dinner and hangs out with in public. My friend? Well, they have a lot of sex, wild sex even, but never has he taken her to dinner in their hometown. She had to fly to another country, on her dime, to get a public dinner out of him. But she keeps playing the other-woman game because, in her mind, someday she will *win* and this guy will be hers. She will beat the girlfriend, and finally she will be with the love of her life, for-ever. Maybe so. Maybe not. After five years, the odds are against her.

What is definite is that she can't find the partnership she really wants, because she's in bed with this unavailable man. She won't deal with her own wounds, because this guy keeps her "conveniently" distracted. She also denies the reality that, even if he did pick her, there's no reason to think he would stay faithful to her. Moreover, she won't even consider the fact that he may be sleeping with other women she doesn't know about. And she spends a tremendous amount of energy hating and judging his girl-friend, a woman she doesn't even know.

Many, too many, women find themselves either living a similar scenario or finding pleasure in watching other women's pain on reality TV or their daily soap opera. For some sick reason, many women love drama of this kind. Many of us find satisfaction in winning against other women. We adopt a sense of superiority over them and are gratified by their suffering. And many of us take pleasure in watching women pit themselves against other women on TV. I'm not sure what's sadder, the fact that so many of us eat up reality TV shows and soap operas that portray such things or the true life of a woman in such a situation who puts her life on hold, believing a guy is going to choose her.

But there are three things that I *am* sure of. First, there's no good reason to knowingly sleep with another woman's husband or boyfriend or to stay in a relationship with a man who's continuously unfaithful. Women do it all the time — I've unfortunately been there myself — telling ourselves we do it because of love, strong attraction, destiny, and so on. But the fact is, if you have feelings for a man who's already taken, and it really is "meant to be," you'll meet up again when he's a free agent, and you'll be the better for having waited. Having sex with a guy while he's involved with another woman gives him no motivation to start anything serious with you. And, even if he were to leave her tomorrow, why would you want to be with a man who is so unconscious that he doesn't realize he needs some time on his own to let go of one relationship before he starts another? Even if his relationship is hell, there are reasons he has stayed in it, and these won't go away just because his girlfriend or wife does. This guy has healing to do, and you owe it to yourself to not be a plug for his holes. You also owe it to yourself not to wait around for him to leave. So many women waste their lives waiting for a guy to finally choose them. While they focus on winning him, they walk right by men who could actually be the partners they want. Don't waste a moment of your life. You deserve more.

Which brings us to the second thing I'm sure of. While the reasons we settle for being the other woman are complex — lack of self-confidence, self-esteem, self-love, self-worth, and more — all of them are unhealthy. No one can negate the first point: there is no reason good enough for ever knowingly sleeping with another woman's husband or boyfriend. You are worth more. If you find yourself entangled in such a relationship, I implore you to find the courage to look deeply into yourself and to enlist the help of others — a therapist, healer, spiritual counselor — as you do so. When we're thoroughly entrenched in an unhealthy relationship, we are too tangled up in our own lies and wounds to see clearly. The good news is that you don't have to keep making the same choice over and over again. If you take the first step to ask for help, you take the first step toward the life you really want.

I could write an entire book on the third thing I'm sure of — and maybe someday I will — but for now I'll just point out that we'd all be a lot better off if women stopped competing for men and started supporting each other. Let's get painfully real: When we sleep with another woman's guy, we hurt her directly. We should ask ourselves how we would feel if that "her" was our best friend or sister — or ourselves! When we watch reality TV shows that pit women against women, we are reveling in other women's suffering. I challenge all of us to ask ourselves, "What inside ME am I so unable to look at that I need to revel in the suffering of other women?" When we engage in any action, no matter how passive or direct, in which we act as perpetrator of or witness to another woman's pain, we assume — and perpetuate — the role of catty, backstabbing bitch. I dare us — all women — to find a better way to relate to one another, a way based on love and respect, if for no other reason than we have all had a lot of the same experiences, and frankly, we could use each other's wisdom and friendship.

❤ ME Reflections ❤

- Have you ever been the other woman? What were your beliefs about the situation that kept you in it? What was true and what were the lines of bull you fed yourself?
- Have you ever watched a friend be the other woman? If so, how did you judge her? What can you learn about yourself from her experience?
- When have you made unhealthy choices regarding men because of your own low self-esteem or low self-confidence? What are three choices you'd never make again? And what are the choices you'd make instead?
- When have you pitted yourself against another woman? When have you judged another woman or found joy or entertainment in her pain? What did you get from it? If you look honestly at your relationships with other women — whether they are friends, co-workers, or women you see on TV — what would you like to be different?

Delving Deeper
DITCH YOUR ROLE AS VICTIM. TAKE RESPONSIBILITY. IT'S TIME TO LIVE IN TRUTH.

Unwavering, uncompromising honesty demands from every woman that she relinquish the role of victim and accept total accountability for her life, including her relationships. What do we get in exchange? The freedom to make our dreams real. Shackled to our own self-deceptions, we cannot, under any circumstances, have what our heart desires. Instead we just keep creating reflections of our lies and their corresponding fears, and we usually end up feeling like a victim or a martyr, depending on our preferred brand of self-pity. But when we stop playing victim and start taking responsibility, we see that we've created our own suffering, and that we can make different choices based on truth, choices that do create what we actually desire.

One of the most catalyzing moments of my life occurred when a teacher conveyed the following wisdom to me, which changed my entire perspective on how my ex-person ended things: People are who they are. When you believe a person to be something else, you get hurt and angry and feel deceived. The fact is, while a man's actions or words may hurt, you're the one who saw him as someone other than who he really was. It's all about expectations. Whatever actions someone takes are likely to be totally congruent with who he really is, not who you imagine him to be. Yes, this guy may have done or said some crappy things, but if you're honest about the real HE, is that such a surprise? Stop being a victim! Take responsibility for your reality.

When I finally heard these words — I mean *heard* them, so that the sound penetrated every cell in my body — my life shifted forever. This was eight months after my breakup, and although happy to be free, I was still extremely hurt by my ex's actions and words. I was also firmly planted in victimhood, which let me blame everything on him and get the sympathy I deserved! However, I began to realize that, while I remained a victim, the hurting never stopped, no matter how much empathy came my way. I was in a continuous loop, feeling rejected, feeling unlovable, and feeling I had done something wrong.

When at last I understood that *I* was the real perpetrator —
because I had been unwilling to see the truth — I really *got* how
I created my reality. I'd *let* my fiancé lie to me, cheat on me, and,
finally, pull the rug from beneath me. He had lied before, and I had
made excuses; he had said he wasn't ready to get married, so I had
pressured him to propose; I hadn't liked who he was becoming, so
I'd pretended it wasn't happening. We were both unhappy, but
couldn't communicate; we were both immature, but couldn't
responsibly end our relationship. If I had opened my eyes and seen
who he was, instead of seeing the man I wanted him to be, it would
have been no surprise when he broke off our engagement. Heck,
I would have beaten him to it! But I clung to a fantasy just to keep
the relationship going.

The most painful part was acknowledging that I had lied to
myself. *I* sold Christine out and in the process created my own suffering. Coming to terms with this was agonizing, as it sent me
through the painful (and long) process of forgiving *myself* — for
being a victim, for disrespecting and dishonoring myself, and
for turning my back on *my* dreams. Forgiving my ex was a piece
of cake compared to forgiving myself. Forgiving him required
acceptance and compassion; forgiving me — well, that demanded
taking 100 percent responsibility for what I had ultimately done
to myself.

How ready are you to be completely honest about your life and
relationships? Can you leave behind your lies, regardless of the
consequences? Are you ready for full responsibility, free of any
traces of victimhood? Let's delve deeper and find out! First, we'll
uncover any victimlike patterns and stories you've got hanging
around. Second, we'll take time to transform at least one of those
victim tales into an epic of empowerment. And lastly, you'll have
the chance to make a commitment to yourself that could change
your life.

Uncovering the Victim

- List all the ways in which you've felt like a victim in your relationships. What are the common themes? As you answer the following questions, notice what other themes emerge.

- When have you chosen to see your guy as someone other than who he truly is? Maybe you had expectations he could not consistently meet that left you feeling bad or mad. Or maybe you found yourself often saying things like, "If he would just..." or "Why can't he just...?" or "I can't believe he..." How did this take away your power or otherwise keep you from getting what you wanted for yourself?

- When have you let yourself be treated with anything less than total respect and love? Why, in all honesty, did you sell yourself out? Remember, there is nothing to feel ashamed about; we've all done it. And we can all start making different choices anytime we choose.

- Where else in your life — at work, with family, with friends, in your handling of money, in school — have you let yourself feel like a victim? What's the pattern?

Exercise: AN EPIC OF EMPOWERMENT
What's Your Story?

- Write down one of your relationship experiences, from start to finish, in which you honestly felt like a victim. Tell your story as a victim of the circumstances in which you found yourself, and describe what influenced you to behave as you did. Read it aloud.

- Now write or tell the same story from a perspective of total responsibility, in which you hold yourself accountable for everything. Challenge yourself to keep the story totally free of victim storylines. Acknowledge that you created this reality. Read the story aloud.

Choose Your New Story

- What do you notice about how the two stories make you feel? Which one empowers you? Which one takes something from you? Which one tells the story of the woman you want to be? Choose the story you want to live and tell from this day forward.
- Look back at all your previous and current relationships in which you saw yourself as a victim, in which you often made excuses or blamed others for your circumstances, or in which you otherwise didn't take responsibility for your reality. How can you take responsibility for what happened?
- Look back at all the information you supplied in the "Uncovering the Victim" section. Now consider these questions: What do you *want* to forgive yourself for? What *will* you forgive yourself for now?

Dare to Commit to Truth

Trading in the burden of victimhood for the badge of full responsibility starts with a very specific commitment to one's self: absolute honesty all the time. I like to think of this commitment as a vow, because it is as serious, if not more so, than any promise we would ever make to a man. I invite you to take a vow of self-honesty.

To get you started, I'm including the vow I wrote for myself. Every woman has to find her own words, a statement that reflects the promise that lives in her heart and soul, something that signals the level of commitment she is willing and ready to make to herself.

◎ A VOW TO ME AND HONESTY ◎

I vow to always be honest with ME, to never hide from the truth, no matter what. I commit to unwavering, uncompromising truth about myself and with myself.

Spend some time writing out the precise vow that you intend to keep. Practice it aloud a few times. When you are ready to commit to the real deal, do something special like lighting a candle and taking a few minutes to get centered. State your commitment out loud with confidence: "I vow to..." Let the vow and the feeling of your words soak into your body, mind, and soul.

CHAPTER *Three*

Loving ME

Do I Really Love ME, All of Her?

WHAT THIS MEANS AND WHAT IT TAKES

One of the most difficult, most essential, most fabulous, fantastic, and absolutely powerful things every woman, every last one of us, must do in her lifetime is fall in love with herself, for exactly who she is, every last bit of her. As you can tell, I am exuberant, excited, and unabashed in my feelings on this topic. *Must* is not a word I use often, but when it comes to loving yourself, unequivocally it is something every woman *must* do. Why, you may ask, am I so adamant about this loving-yourself business? Because if I know one thing for sure, it's that when our choices, beliefs, and commitments are grounded in a complete love of self, *everything* in life falls into place. We make decisions and create realities that support what *we*, not everyone else around us, really want from life. We are able to fully express, instead of repress, our most authentic selves. And, we finally stop settling for less.

Too many of us spend our energy complaining about our relationships or pining away for a partner who unconditionally loves us, when what we really need is to focus on ourselves. If we don't love ME first, no amount of hoping or harping will change our situations. Creating a healthy, loving partnership starts with the love we have for ourselves. When we deeply respect and unwaveringly love ME, any relationship that doesn't reflect the same will not survive. We won't let it. Think about someone you deeply love. Would you ever let anything repeatedly hurt or sadden him or her? Most of us would protect that person, would demand something better for him or her. Loving ourselves should be no different. Too often, however, it is.

Most women don't love themselves, not really. The majority of us never step out of our busy lives long enough to even get what loving ourselves means. Nor do we talk about it with our girlfriends, mothers, or daughters; read about it in our favorite magazines; or see it featured on our favorite television shows. Think about it. When was the last time you asked, "Do I truly love myself?" Odds are, probably not recently, if ever. The thought never crossed my mind until I began looking at myself for answers to how I ended up in an unhappy fifteen-year relationship that kept me settling for less, instead of living the life my heart and spirit desired.

When my life came to a screeching halt after my ex-person left, I was forced to look honestly at my illusions about myself and my relationship. I didn't want to repeat the experience, but I didn't know exactly how to prevent this. What I came to learn was that it was as easy — and as hard — as learning to love Christine, both for who she is today and for who she was in the past. I ended up with an understanding of how my lack of self-love had created my reality — a concept no one had ever shared with me.

Although it took me a few years to figure out how to live a life grounded in self-love, you can start seeing immediate results yourself. Once you start down the road to discovering what loving ME really means, life starts to change. To get started, ask yourself the following three questions. These inquiries became guideposts and helped me ensure that I was indeed loving ME first. We'll explore them in detail, but for now just read each one aloud, stop, and notice what, if any, answers arise.

1. DO I LOVE ME, ALL OF ME, COMPLETELY, ALL THE TIME?
   (I'm not talking about self-esteem or liking yourself, but deep, unwavering love of yourself.)

2. AM I COMMITTED TO *MY* HAPPINESS?
   (That is, not everyone else's, but yours.)

3. HOW DO MY ACTIONS AND BELIEFS SUPPORT MY AN-SWERS? OR DO THEY CONTRADICT THEM?
   (No bull, is what you're doing actually making you happy?)

I have to admit that, when these questions first occurred to me, I didn't like my honest answers. For thirty years, I'd believed that I loved ME, but the truth was that I didn't really. I liked myself a lot in many ways, yes. Truckloads of self-esteem? Check. But real self-love, no way! I hadn't a clue what that even was. However, if anyone had asked me, "Are you committed to your happiness? Do you love yourself?" I would have bellowed, "Yes!" And it would have been an absolute lie. Because of my lack of self-awareness and my fear, I would have been oblivious to my self-deceit.

A successful woman by society's standards, I really believed that I'd been guided by a drive for my own happiness. I'd always been secure in who I was and believed that I could do anything. I almost always went for what I wanted, and I usually got it. I could have been the poster child for self-esteem. But having never stopped to ask myself, "Are you happy? Does your life really reflect unconditional love for Christine?" I didn't recognize that my life, especially my relationship with the man I loved, was shredding my soul. Unable to see that I didn't love myself, I made some really bad decisions for Christine. Looking back, I'm sure that facing the truth was too much to handle, so I just kept propelling myself forward, letting myself believe I was living the life I wanted. Ha!

Being honest about how well our choices reflect our love and respect for self can be difficult for women. Of course, we don't want to admit that we don't love ourselves or don't make choices that bring us happiness. At the same time, most of us also won't publicly announce, "Hey everybody, I am in love with ME!" or "My happiness is a top priority!"

Laden with the belief that loving ourselves is selfish, we choose to accept that we are *supposed to* selflessly give our love, energy, and time to everyone else *first* — leaving little, if any, left over for us. Generations of women have passed along this philosophy, not because they benefited, but because society supports it. Women give and give and give until nothing remains; we compromise our needs and wants in order to take care of others, and we end up empty, frustrated, and dissatisfied. We buy into the martyr role, believing our sacrifices are the only way to give, to love, and to be "good women."

As I began to understand the power of talking about and finding self-love and happiness, I got excited. Finally, the key to freeing ourselves from self-created misery. With unabashed exuberance I shared my newfound revelations with other women, asking, "Are you in love with yourself? Will you choose ME before WE and put your own happiness first?" I was depressed by the responses. Almost always, women's answers demonstrated that they were weighed down by the heavy, time-honored bags of guilt and selflessness — like the ones I had carried myself.

Some women quickly answered "yes," almost as a reflex, sounding very sure and clearly wanting to change the conversation. Like me, when I first started asking myself these questions, they didn't want to face the truth. To my surprise, others practically stopped breathing. Upon recovering their composure, they would launch into a defense of selflessness and sacrifice complete with the opinion that self-love was selfish, narcissistic, and unrealistic. Arrgh! I was disheartened and saddened. Why were so many women vehemently unwilling to love themselves? Why were they protecting beliefs that kept them stuck in such unhappiness? Thankfully my despair was alleviated whenever I met women who paused to reflect when questioned. The answers these women gave spoke the truth of their experience. Yes, they wanted to love themselves; some had learned to, and most believed that all women needed to. These women were exuberant about the possibility of every woman and girl loving herself.

Until we *consciously* seek a different perspective on self-love, loving ourselves and finding our own happiness will seem difficult, unimportant, and selfish, maybe even impossible — and that is the undeniable truth! The good news is, each of us has the power to choose ME, to make self-love and happiness a nonnegotiable part of being a woman. It's time we redefine what loving ME means. Guilt and sacrifice are part of the old story. The new story tells us that loving ME is the most generous, life-giving act we can undertake on behalf of ourselves and every person our lives touch. The more we love ME, the more we can give to WE — without depleting our spirits and life force. When we are cared for, healed, loved, and fulfilled, we have energy to share with the people we love. It's like the safety rules you've heard over and over on airplanes: In case of emergency, put *your* air mask on *first*, before attempting to assist anyone else. If you pass out because you can't breathe, you can't help anyone. Loving ourselves is actually an act of selflessness, not selfishness.

Falling in Love with ME: What It Means

Falling in love with ME is a journey, an active adventure that touches every aspect of our lives. So vast and deep, the concept of loving one's self can be hard to wrap our heads around. So let me give it to you in the simplest terms possible. Loving yourself completely is the unwavering commitment to and active expression of

1. knowing yourself;
2. accepting yourself;
3. living as the fullest expression of your real ME in all parts of your life; and
4. attracting and allowing into your life only people and situations that support all of the above.

Just to be clear, it's not a linear path in which these four statements equate to "four easy to steps to loving yourself." Falling in love with one's self doesn't happen overnight or even in the course of a few months. It occurs through the collective power of a series of small things — actions, beliefs, realizations, and experiences — and this love will continue to increase for the rest of your life, if you let it.

While each of us has a unique path and will find many ways to deepen and express our love of ME, there are some common ways of being, doing, and seeing that go on the "must-have" list for self-love. I've included some here to get you started. As you read them, reflect honestly on how much they do or do not describe your relationship with yourself.

Loving ME: A Sampling of What It Takes

BE YOUR OWN BEST FRIEND. Love hanging out with you. When you are deeply connected to ME, there's no reason to fear being alone. Honestly believe the following: "I would rather be companionless than with others who take away from how great I feel about ME, whether this refers to family, friends, or a man."

SEE YOUR MAGNIFICENCE AND BEAUTY. Embrace the amazing woman you are every day. Let everyone around you see her too. Cherish your own brilliance, without reserve or fear of it being greater than someone else's light. The more radiant you are, the more others will be inspired to show their own splendor.

LOVE ALL OF YOURSELF, EVEN THE NOT-SO-PRETTY PARTS. Accept your flaws, idiosyncrasies, and weaknesses. Love yourself for who you have been and are. Forgive yourself for decisions that were not self-supporting. Acknowledge the dark parts of your life and spirit, and love them just as they are.

MAKE DECISIONS GUIDED BY SELF-LOVE. Take actions only if they uphold your commitment to self. Always be honest about how a relationship or other situation adds to or detracts from loving ME. And if you can't be honest with yourself, ask a trusted friend to advise you — and actually listen to what this person says.

CHANGE YOUR PERSPECTIVE ON BELIEFS THAT COUNTER SELF-LOVE. Tell those negative voices in your head to take a hike, throw the "shoulds" into the garbage, and leave the bags of guilt at the door. Be willing to believe in the possibility of new possibilities, ones that breed and nourish love.

NEVER APOLOGIZE FOR WHO YOU ARE. Believe that your choices, made with integrity and love, never have to be justified to anyone else. Be confident in who you are, and never let anyone say you should be someone else.

MAKE UNCONDITIONAL LOVE A REQUIREMENT FOR ALL RELATIONSHIPS. Keep only the relationships with people — partners, friends, and family — who accept, love, and support you for you. They don't have to always like, agree with, or understand your choices, or you theirs, but love in the relationship must be unwavering. Do not have relationships with people who cannot love you as you are today, whose love is conditional and inconsistent. If you aren't getting unconditional love from someone you'd like to remain in your life, be willing to ask for it and to be honest about how they can give it.

GIVE AND RECEIVE. One of the best parts of loving ME is getting to love other people too. Love others freely, without expectation, resentment, or attachment to the outcome.

This is not a comprehensive list but a starting point. I follow all these guidelines myself and can attest to the miraculous shift loving ME can make in life. Use these guidelines to help yourself discover what loving ME really means for you.

Falling in Love with ME: What It Takes

I'm not going to lie to you and say that loving yourself is as easy as proclaiming, "Yes! I love myself!" The journey of falling in love with ME takes place over time, your entire lifetime, really. Often, falling in love with one's self is exhilarating and liberating. It can also be difficult and painful. It always requires honesty, and sometimes this means making hard choices that may hurt at the time but are needed to transform your reality.

Over the course of my own journey, I've done some wacky things, and I've made some decisions that were unpopular with others, but that's what it takes. Loving yourself requires you to step out of your comfort zone; it requires you to listen to and live from your heart and soul. Following are some of the actions I've taken to honestly love ME. I like to think of them as adventures in self-love, or as dares that push us beyond what's comfortable into what's possible. In fact, just to liven things up for myself, inspired by the game of Truth or Dare we used to play as kids, I upped the ante and challenged myself to "Truth *and* Dare." What do you think? Do you dare to be, love, and live you? Try these yourself.

TRUTH: I see my magnificence and beauty.
DARE: Give yourself love, out loud!
ACTION: Every morning, before you do anything else, find a mirror, look deeply into your eyes, and exclaim with gusto, "I love you!" Follow it with a giant, tight, loving hug. Then, at some point during the morning (before work), do the "I love ME!" mantra. Tell yourself out loud, with utter adoration and passion, "I love [insert your name here]!" Do this fifty times a day.

I have to admit that, although it's a magnificent way to start the day, when I first tried this loving-yourself-in-the-mirror thing, I honestly felt awkward and a little foolish. Looking oneself squarely in the eyes, seeing deeply inside and sending pure love, is difficult, not to mention bizarre. But I got used to it and started to enjoy seeing myself and letting the energy of love sink in. Luckily, I lived alone, so no one, other than my dog, Nanook, thought I had lost my mind! Eventually, to do my fifty "I love Christine!" affirmations, I got courageous and left the safety of my bathroom and took to the sidewalks of Chicago, morning and evening. While walking Nanook, I recited, "I love Christine!" fifty times, twice a day. People did occasionally stare, especially as I got more comfortable with the thought of loving ME, and my words turned into jingles and, on special days, full-on ballads. I didn't care, and neither did Nanook. The affirmations were helping, my belief patterns began to shift, and I loved being free to express how much I really *did* love ME!

TRUTH: You are your own best friend.
DARE: Take yourself out on best-friend dates.

ACTION: Think about the things you really love to do and often feel compelled to invite other people to do with you, or that you don't do because there isn't someone to do them with. Make a date with yourself. Get ready for the date, spending time to get yourself all beautiful, just as you would for a man. Escort yourself on the date — really be present with you the entire time, like you are having the experience of being on the date *and* watching it as an observer. Notice how you're feeling and reacting to things throughout the date. Look at yourself from the outside in, seeing your beauty and what is unique about who you are (just as a man would adoringly look at you). Be with yourself. And if you're feeling really spunky, talk to yourself throughout the night!

As my love for ME intensified, I went from being a girl who couldn't do anything alone (even an excursion to a convenience store required a companion) to being a woman who adored herself and loved spending time connecting with her inner magnificence. I took myself to dinners, movies, and art shows and on long walks. Slowly, I began not only to love ME but also to really like ME, at a level much deeper than I had ever thought existed. Three years after my first date with Christine, I went on my first overnight trip, alone, for the sole purpose of connecting to myself. Of course, I had been away before, but always with other people or for business. This time it was just ME. I remember the luxurious featherbed, the romantic dinner seated by the inn's fireplace, and the decadent dessert I had delivered by room service. The small, elegant restaurant in Northern California's wine country had been filled with couples, except for me, and I felt completely at home, enjoying my own company and experiencing every bite of food as a delectable discovery. That night was one of the first times I can remember knowing that my strong affection for myself had transformed into true love.

TRUTH: Unconditional love is a requirement for all relationships.

DARE: Settle for nothing less than unconditional love in all relationships.

ACTION: Examine all your relationships. Which ones support you in loving the woman you are today, all of her? Which ones don't? Consider each one that doesn't, and get clear on what you want from the other person in the relationship. Be honest about what this person can give you, and ask for what you want. If he or she can't give it, end the relationship or establish a new boundary.

This action was one of the hardest, not because it was difficult to expect unconditional love — love without restrictions or conditions — from my partner, and, for that matter, from anyone I consider a friend or part of my family, but because our society has rules that tell us to accept restrictions and conditions, and people don't like it when you push against those. We're told, "Family is family," "You've known her your whole life, so you can't end the friendship," "Buck up and take it; he's not so bad," or "You have to take the bad with the good." And we're told that these are unchangeable truths. It tends not to occur to us that we have a *choice*, and that we need not explain ourselves to anyone. The only being we owe justification to is our self.

Sometimes we have to break ties with people we love, and this can be hard. Because we love them, we don't want to end the relationship — especially when it comes to lovers and partners. But if we're committed to loving ourselves, all the people who tear down our self-esteem, self-confidence, and well-being have to go. Even relationships that, while not overtly destructive or abusive, keep us from living the lives we really desire, or prevent us from fully expressing our truest selves, may have to be limited or severed. And in most instances, this doesn't happen easily. We don't want to admit that, if we're going to continue to grow, the relationship must end.

Sometimes our partners get in the way of our finding unconditional love for ourselves, and we think, "My guy loves me, so why wouldn't he want me to my best ME? Why wouldn't he want me to be 100 percent happy?" In truth, many people who don't want to change feel threatened when the people around them start growing or trading in limiting beliefs for self-loving ones. In such circumstances, a man may resist, become indifferent, or threaten to leave. Such behaviors have nothing to do with love or your happiness — they are about him. He may be scared to death that you won't need him once you love yourself. Or he may fear that the spotlight will be turned on his own lack of self-love, and since he doesn't want to change himself, he won't want you to change either. You deserve people in your life that support the woman you are today and are growing into. However, you'll have to be ready to be honest. Just because you wake up and decide to hop on the path to loving ME doesn't mean your partner will be ready too — and you have to be willing to move on without him.

My ex-person, who was light-years away from loving himself, told me at the end of our relationship that he thought I didn't need him any longer. And he was right! I was in the beginning stages of learning to love ME, which should have been a great addition to our relationship. Instead, my growing connection to and expression of my true ME freaked him out, and ultimately it contributed to his hasty departure. His conditional love was based on conditional need, which I started to really understand once I began to heal after our union ended. Then the question was clear: "Do I want to be with a man who doesn't fully support me in loving myself, someone who may not love himself?" The answer was a roaring "no!"

❤ ME Reflections ❤

Do you truly love yourself today? "Not yet" is an okay answer. In fact, most of us don't honestly love ourselves, unless we have made a conscious choice and put a heck of a lot of effort into doing so. Use this reflection time as a check in, to find out where you are on your journey to loving yourself. Remember, it's not a linear process that you mark with numbers, percentages, or grades. It's much more about noticing when and how you compromise your true self, and then taking steps to know, accept, and express her instead.

- Look back at the different decades in your life and notice how you've evolved as a woman. What about yourself do you really love today? How is this different from in the past? Notice how hard or easy it is for you to embrace what's great about you. Loving yourself means celebrating yourself.

- What about yourself don't you like, are you ashamed of, or do you regret? Certain past experiences or mistakes? Habits? Physical, emotional, or mental aspects? Will you love these pieces of yourself too, exactly as they are today? Loving yourself means accepting *all* of you.

- How do you downplay your talents or push away compliments? When have you apologized for who you are? Felt unworthy or not good enough and shrunk back to hide the real you? Loving yourself means expressing the fullest you.

- Think about relationships you've kept — with men, women, friends, family — that didn't support you in loving yourself for yourself, 24/7. These can range from the obvious — abusive, self-destructive, dramatic, disrespectful relationships — to the more subtle ones that feel

obligatory or that require you to give too much of yourself or tolerate behaviors that affect you negatively. What
effect did or do they have on you? What keeps you from
changing them? What empowered choices can you make?
Loving yourself means having only relationships that
don't take more than they give to you.

Loving ME is a journey that takes time, and for most of us it's
a foreign concept that introduces new feelings, experiences, beliefs,
and proclamations. So it makes sense that the road to finding self-
love looks a little murky. This is where the happiness gauge can
help us.

The Happiness Gauge

One way to measure how well we are doing on our journey to love
ME is to take pause, reflect on our relationships or life situations,
and ask, "Am I happy?" This question works well in large part
because it's about no one else but you and how happy *you* feel.
Most of us can easily tell if we're happy or not. But unfortunately,
most of us never stop running through life long enough to ask,
"Am *I* really happy?" And in the rare instances when we do
reflect, the reply is likely anything but honest, mainly because we
don't like the true answer.

How many times have you been unwilling to admit your
unhappiness to anyone else, or even to yourself? Have you ever
lied about being unhappy or simply avoided the question altogether
because you couldn't deal with the reality? We've all done it,
probably too many times to count. And the truth is, we can't do
that anymore if we ever hope to create the lives we really want.

Whether it's your life or your relationship, having what you
truly desire requires your commitment to both self-love and
happiness. Like Siamese twins, one always comes with the other.
Without self-love, we put our happiness in the hands of others, and

we will bend and shift according to their whims, needs, and influence. Without a commitment to *our* own happiness, we sacrifice and compromise ourselves, and while we may win the approval of others or even satisfy their desires, our happiness gets left out in the cold.

Choosing your own happiness inevitably requires some difficult decisions and a fair amount of work to shift old patterns, beliefs, and behaviors. We've been trained to settle for less, put others first without regard for ourselves, act out of obligation, and be overly modest — and, by the way, doing any of these things is the antithesis of loving ME. Choosing your happiness also requires you to honor the commitment you made to maintain unwavering and uncompromising honesty with yourself. I know from experience that it's way too easy to lie to yourself when a difficult choice or a tantalizing distraction shows up, or when the truth seems too hard to deal with.

I've watched women accept the challenge to fall in love with themselves with every intention of following through, but then, within weeks, they attract a situation, many times a relationship, that is so *not* about loving themselves. I'll ask, "How's your adventure of loving yourself going?" Almost always, the reply, regardless of the truth, is: "Great. I'm doing great." A woman may tell me this even if she's just entered into yet another relationship that disregards her self-respect, she's accepted a family obligation she wants nothing to do with, or she's taken a job that is totally unaligned with what she wants and who she truly is. It's way too easy to fool ourselves when we don't want to see the truth. That's where the happiness question comes in. It's an instant truth detector, a gauge for happiness. When I ask a woman enmeshed in a situation in which she is not loving herself, "Are you really happy?" and "Do your actions and beliefs reflect that?" she may muster up a "yes," but never with confidence. The truth almost always surfaces, and while the situation may not immediately resolve itself, she becomes a lot clearer about what loving herself is and is not.

Cora's Story

I shared my happiness gauge with my friend Cora to help shed light on her self-inflicted misery, which derived from an unfulfilling relationship of her choosing. Cora had already agreed that she needed to learn to love Cora. In therapy, reading self-help books, and journaling, she was making progress, albeit slowly, on the self-love front. For a woman who achieved everything else faster than average, her journey to loving ME was moving at a snail's pace, and for one reason — a man.

Cora had been dating, and had fallen in love with, an unavailable man, Jerod. Playing two sides of the bed, Cora's and his girlfriend's, all Jerod could offer Cora was great sex and a surface-level friendship. He never promised her more. But convinced that their love would prevail, Cora still desperately believed that someday Jerod would choose her over his girlfriend. No amount of reasoning made a dent in Cora's unwavering attachment to Jerod. She couldn't admit that the relationship was demeaning, and, worse, that it did nothing to help Cora love herself.

The tables turned when we started talking about happiness. For a while, Cora had been happy to settle for whatever she could get from Jerod, but now what he offered wasn't enough. She was no longer happy. She couldn't deny how sad and awful she felt when she woke up alone in the morning after a late night of steamy physical connection. She was jealous of couples in love who could be seen together in public. Once Cora recognized just how unhappy she was, she could — and did! — decide it was time to choose herself before the relationship. For the first time, Cora's happiness became a priority over Jerod's. Cora approached Jerod about her unhappiness, and still he offered no more than to continue on his terms. Cora ended their relationship and, like the true rock star she is, catapulted light-years ahead on her journey to loving ME. Cora is happier and is also beginning to understand that she has the power to create joy in her life by the choices she makes.

I encourage you to use the question "Am I happy?" as a barometer, and then to ask the question "Do my actions and beliefs really support my answer?" Especially when we are just starting out, the concept of self-love can seem nebulous. But happiness — we really know what that does or doesn't feel like. Think about how you feel when you're happy. Go beyond the feeling of having a smile on your face, to that deep tingling sensation in your heart and soul. And then remember what it's like when that happiness is gone or some other feeling, like anger, anxiety, or despair, is present. It's hard to mistake one of those for happiness.

Happiness: A State of Being, Not an Emotion

There is one thing about happiness that we often get confused: the distinction between the emotion of happiness and the state of true happiness. Let me preface my discussion of it by saying that there are hundreds of books written on the pursuit of happiness, spiritual traditions founded on it, and gurus around the world teaching it. I am not about to launch into a discussion of the meaning of life, but I do feel it's important to point to the difference between the emotion and the state of happiness so you can read the "Am I happy?" gauge with accuracy.

The simplest way I can put this is: True happiness does not mean walking around with big grins on our faces every moment of every day. The truth is, we have many emotions that don't make us smile — sadness, worry, and fear, to name a few. When an event brings those feelings forth, a smile can seem a million miles away. And that's okay. Emotions are not good or bad. They just are. They come and go every minute of every day, and our job is only to have them, notice them, make choices, and let them go.

The emotion of happiness is not what we measure with the "Am I happy?" gauge. When you reflect on your happiness, I want you to feel your overall state of being, to reach a much deeper sense of joy in your heart and soul, the kind that can be found even when life is hard. It's a feeling of being fulfilled no matter what's happening on the outside. This kind of happiness is neither temporary nor dependent on changes in our environment; it's either within you or it isn't. Either you have a sense of fulfillment in your life, or you don't, and relationships are often large contributing factors.

My journey to knowing this kind of happiness and fulfillment started with the realization that *I* was responsible for my unhappiness, and that I had no clue about where real happiness came from. By all external accounts, my happiness meter should have pointed to overload once I became free of my toxic, unfulfilling relationship. After all, I had achieved a ton of material success and had a promising career, a top-level education, and a decent bank account. My friends were supportive, and they deeply cared about me. I was involved with a wonderful man who was kind, generous, considerate, and charismatic, not to mention the fact that he liked me for who I was. I had more than most do, yet I yearned for more. It's more accurate, really, to say I was really yearning for "other," not more.

Eventually I realized I had been looking for true happiness in all the wrong places — outside myself. The strong center I sought existed only inside my connection to myself (my soul) and to a force bigger than my ego, society, and the planet: my faith in and connection to providence, the divine, the universe, or whatever you want to call it. It is the place of true faith and the trust that, no matter what, everything is going to be okay. It is knowing that, although we may love our designer shoes and BMWs, they don't determine our happiness. Our joy and love come from knowing what's really important to ME and then living a life that reflects it. They come from the connection to self, both body and spirit, and to the freedom to fully, without holding back, express our truest selves. How we each discover this, and how we each experience it, will differ; but if we want happiness, we each have to find it.

♥ ME Reflections ♥

- Do your relationships — with your partner, friends, and family — make you happy? Close your eyes and see yourself connecting with each of the people in your life. How do you feel when you're around them? After you've spent time with them? Notice when you feel energized and alive, and when you feel drained or sad. What does this tell you about your happiness?

- If you answered yes to being happy in your relationships, how do your actions and beliefs actually support that fact? How are they incongruent?

- If you answered no, what are the biggest sources of your unhappiness? Why have you let yourself stay unhappy? What's the victim story? What's the empowered-self story? What would change in your life if you altered your relationship(s)? What are three steps you can take to make the change?

Our Choice

In the end, if we don't decide that loving ourselves is a priority, then, rest assured, no one else will. If we don't make our own happiness as important as everyone else's, it will get shoved aside. When we choose ME over guilt and sacrifice, we have the power to claim our self-love and happiness every day. And with that choice, anything is possible. Not only can we create fantastically rewarding lives for ourselves, but we can also experience the joy of giving and receiving unconditional love. Every woman deserves to be utterly in love with herself and to have complete happiness in her life. Don't ever let anyone, not even yourself — especially not yourself! — tell you differently.

Delving Deeper
WHAT'S INFLUENCING ME?

As I've mentioned, the journey to self-love is not a one-two-three-step plan. And like any change we make in ourselves, it's always easier to deal with the most obvious areas in need of shift. Becoming our true selves is like peeling an onion: We keep peeling the layers until we get to the core. Self-love and happiness already exist at the center of our beings; we just need to strip off the layers prohibiting us from accessing them.

I've discussed removing some of the barriers to self-love, but there are more to go. Let's explore some of the layers lurking beneath the surface by examining the ideals, thoughts, and preconceived notions — both conscious and subconscious — you may have about loving yourself or making your happiness a priority above others'. Our lives are constantly influenced by the images, opinions, attitudes, and beliefs that surround us from birth to death. By shedding light on these forces, we can better understand whose thoughts are *really* driving our decisions and points of view. If we are to be fully responsible for our lives, we must clearly distinguish between others' ideals and our own. Only then will we be free to create the lives our souls want. Are you willing to see what's been influencing you, so that you can make *conscious choices*? If so, let's dive in.

Exercise: THE RESTRUCTURING WHEEL

Before we jump in to action, I'll point out that what follows is not an exercise I dreamed up or learned at a weekend workshop. I'm about to take you on a journey into something called the Restructuring Wheel, one of many medicine wheels based on the deep wisdom of indigenous peoples and used to help us see into our lives from different perspectives. I learned about this wheel from my teacher Pele Rouge, a woman who looks just like you and me but who has spent years studying and who now carries the ancient Earth Wisdom Teachings of the people of the Ehama Institute. I've taken journeys via the Restructuring Wheel myself many times, and every time, I've come out with something I couldn't see before. I invite you to pursue the same possibility for yourself.

To begin, get a few pieces of blank paper and something to write with. On the first sheet, draw a big circle in the center that fills up most of the page, leaving an inch or two open along the edges. Inside the center of the circle, write the words *Self-Love* and *Putting My Happiness First*. Now envision the circle as a compass, and label the four directions: north, south, west, and east. On the north part of the circle, aka the top, write the word *Beliefs*. In the west, write *Attitudes*; in the south, or bottom, write *Opinions*; and in the east, write *Images*. You are about to dive deeply into the four areas of influence — the images, opinions, attitudes, and beliefs that affect your ability to love yourself and to put your happiness first.

Uncovering the Images, Opinions, Attitudes, and Beliefs Influencing ME

As you explore each of these four areas of influence, remember that this is an expedition to uncover what is affecting — sometimes consciously but more often subconsciously — your perceptions of and ideas about *self-love* and *happiness*.

As you prepare to approach each direction, first look at the center of the circle and read aloud the words you've written there. Then come back to the book and, starting in the east, with the "Images" section, read the paragraph about it from beginning to end. Then reread the questions in the paragraph about images, one at a time, pausing between each one to let yourself think about events in your past, as well as those in your present. Really get into the questions, and when you're ready, on a separate piece of paper write down everything that comes to mind in response to them. Use as many pieces of paper as you need. Do not censor yourself; do not think too much; do not strive for the "right" answers. Open up the floodgates and let the words flow, capturing everything that arises. Think of it as a brainstorm: there are no right or wrong answers. These are for your personal viewing only, so challenge yourself. Even when you feel as if you've exhausted all thoughts, keep going. There are always more, and many times the best thoughts come out at the end. Your goal is to end up with a thorough list of responses to questions about each of the four areas of influence.

Once you've finished with "Images," move along the

wheel clockwise to the next section, "Opinions" (south), and so on until you've finished all four areas of influence, ending with "Beliefs" (north).

Images

The images in our heads come from the media and popular culture. Thinking about images of self-love and personal happiness, remember the shows you've seen on television, movies you've watched, or music you've listened to, either in recordings or in concert. Think of famous people or significant role models. Remember current or past events, foreign or domestic, and the people involved. What visual representations surface? Scan your lifetime from your early youth to today. What, and who, comes to mind when you think about women or men loving themselves? About women putting their own happiness first? Write down all the images that appear to you.

Opinions

Our opinions are influenced by our friends. In your teenage years and early twenties, what opinions did you form, based on what your peers thought, about loving yourself and making your happiness a priority? During those formative years, what did you learn about self-love? About making it a point to be happy? What did your friends think? What opinions about happiness and self-love could you freely express? What would have been taboo to think, say, or do? What did you need to believe in order to fit in? Write down all the opinions you can remember.

Attitudes

Our attitudes are influenced by our family. What ideals about loving oneself or putting one's own happiness first did your family either admire or disparage? What attitudes and behaviors were acceptable in your family? Which ones were not? What common phrases did your family members use to express their beliefs about self-love or happiness (for example, "Always put others first" or "Thinking about yourself is selfish")? What familial patterns have caused repeated behaviors throughout multiple generations — in grandmothers, mothers, aunts, and daughters (for example, women play a subservient role in the family, women stay in unhappy marriages, and so on)? Write down all the attitudes that surface.

Beliefs

Beliefs are influenced by formal institutions like school and church. What ideas about self-love and happiness were instilled in you by schools and religious institutions during your early childhood? Teens? Twenties? Thirties and beyond? Often one's beliefs change as one ages (that is, what you believed before you went to college changes after college; or if you were brought up Catholic but became Buddhist later in life, many of your beliefs changed). Write out all the beliefs you were taught and that influenced you along the way, even if you have since discarded them for new ones.

Discovery and Decision

When you've finished, go through your notes and look for three things: First, common themes — the ideas that jump out or come up often. Second, thoughts that disturb you and that you'd like to change. Third, ideals you really like. Circle or underline them. These are the thoughts that influence your self-love and happiness, whether you were previously conscious of them or not.

With these identified, it's time to look honestly at your viewpoints regarding happiness and loving ME. How do they affect your life? Decide which ideals and perspectives you want to keep, and which ones you are ready to let go of or transform. Review the images, opinions, attitudes, and beliefs that you highlighted, and consider the questions in the following two lists.

Discovery

- How do your images, opinions, attitudes, and beliefs drive your decisions and actions? Positively? Negatively?
- How do they prevent you from loving ME? From putting your happiness first?
- How do they support you in loving ME? In making your happiness a priority?
- How do they cause you to avoid certain actions that would help you love yourself more?

Decision

- Which images, opinions, attitudes, and beliefs would you like to keep?
- Which would you like to let go of?
- How can you transform your limiting beliefs into expansive possibilities? One way is to rewrite the thoughts that

no longer serve you into positive statements that support a life of love and happiness — new affirmations! What other actions can you take?

Committing

In the end, loving ME comes down to your willingness to make commitments to yourself and live by them. Sometimes, sticking to these vows requires that we make changes in our relationships and surroundings as well as in ourselves. Making choices may be difficult, the transformations hard, and the realities uncomfortable. But more often than not, when we act from the core of love for self, the outcomes are wonderful beyond our wildest expectations. So I ask *you*, brave, magnificent, and brilliant woman, are you ready to take these vows, remembering that, as with any vow, you can change the wording to fit exactly what comes from your heart and soul?

◎ VOWS OF SELF-LOVE AND HAPPINESS ◎

I, [insert name], make the promise to

- fall more and more in love with myself every day for the rest of my life;
- make my happiness a priority, always; and
- take every action and make every decision with self-love and happiness as my guideposts.

If you are ready to take these vows, great! Just as you did with the honesty vow, find the right words for you, create a sacred space, and state your vow aloud. If you're still not sure that loving ME and choosing your own happiness is a priority, then take some time to sit with the idea. Bring the possibility of loving yourself into your encounters during the next two or three weeks. Try some of the things we've talked about in this chapter. Notice how you and your life change when loving yourself and finding happiness for you are your guideposts. Then come back to the vows of self-love and happiness, and take time to find just the right words for your vow. Make the vow that feels perfect for you.

CHAPTER  *Four*

Trusting ME

Who's That Talking Inside Me?

EMBRACING YOUR INTUITION

Sometimes referred to as a gut feeling, a knowing, or a sixth sense, intuition is undeniably a girl's best friend and a woman's most powerful ally. Intuition puts ME first without exception, "she" never abandons us in our times of need, and, if we learn to trust her, she consistently leads us to truth, even during times of dire uncertainty. Our intuition knows what's best for us — and what's really not — even if we don't think we have a clue. She gives us the honest answers that no one else can and utters warnings when we try to act in ways that don't align with loving ME.

Such a valuable asset, priceless really, but what do most of us do with our intuition? Sadly, we usually ignore her or, even worse, pretend she's not even there. This has to change! Without our intuition, our fears, lies, and illusions win out every time. Without the aid of this keen and centered inner knowing, we're likely to be swayed by others, to settle for less than we deserve, and to hang our own happiness out to dry. You cannot afford to go one more day without learning to trust your wisest and most loyal friend. Your life depends on it.

What Exactly Is Intuition?

Merriam-Webster's Dictionary, eleventh edition, defines *intuition* as "the power or faculty of knowing things without conscious reasoning; quick and ready insight." No wonder we have such a hard time understanding, believing, and trusting intuition — it's not logical, scientific, or easily seen with our eyes. However, this doesn't mean it's not very, very real.

Every living person has intuition. At some point, we've all experienced it — as an inner voice, a sensation, a premonition, or an intense knowing — even if, at the time, we didn't identify it as our "inner guide." Think about an instance when you just knew something was going to happen, such as a specific person calling you on the telephone. One moment, that person popped into your thoughts, and the next minute the phone rang and he or she was on the line saying hello. Of course, you said in return, "I was just thinking about you!" That was your intuition. Intuition is also what makes a mother wake up *before* her baby actually starts to cry. Her inner connection to that child wakes her in preparation for responding to her baby. How many times are mothers asked, "How did you know [insert situation that involves their child]?" and they reply, "I just knew." Of course, they trusted their natural instincts, their intuition, regardless of logic.

But because we cannot see intuition with our eyes or understand it logically, we may discount its relevance and power, even its existence. Even those of us who have consciously experienced its power often continue to doubt it. We have been brainwashed not to trust our own inner knowing. In our logic-based society, admitting to making a decision based on a feeling or an inner voice would be just plain crazy!

I say we have it all mixed up. Dismissing something that can't be explained by logic, despite the fact that it works — now that's demented! If we get great results, why not fully embrace our intuition by learning to trust it and by tapping into its immense power? It's always there, informing us, whether we acknowledge it or not. And the more we access it, the stronger it becomes.

Remember a time when you knew something was right or wrong without any hard evidence? You just "knew." You had a "nagging feeling." A voice spoke to you, one that no one else could hear. Your gut instinct gave her opinion loud and clear — and whether you chose to listen is another story. My friend Carli, for example, heard the words "No! I don't want to marry you!" screaming in her heart and head when her guy proposed. She knew deep inside that she didn't want to marry him. Unfortunately, she didn't listen and, consequently, spent six years in an unhappy marriage and then three years putting herself back together. Think about your own life and the times you knew which action to take, which answer to give, or which words to speak — and not because you had a definitive piece of information. Your knowing was based not on logic but on intuition.

Our inner guide tries to talk to us in many different ways. We may have a knowing or a feeling deep inside. We may hear a voice in our head, as if someone is actually talking to us. Or we may see pictures playing through our mind, whether we're awake or asleep. Our intuition may even try to get our attention with external signs or "coincidences." I don't believe in coincidence. I've learned to trust that anything that seems like a coincidence is actually happening for a reason, and if we listen we can benefit from what it has to teach or give us. For instance, a person we haven't talked to in years happens to reenter our life with something we need. A bus passes by with an advertisement on its side that answers a question we've had in mind. We find ourselves somewhere at just the right time. Too often we brush such occurrences off as chance, when what we should be doing is taking heed of what our intuition is trying to tell us.

❤ ME Reflections ❤

Think about your current connection to your own intuition.

- What is your present relationship with your intuition? Are you intimately connected to it, skilled at listening to it and trusting in it implicitly? Or do you remember times when you just knew something, or heard a voice, or had a dream that seemed to have meaning, but didn't quite know what to do or didn't believe that what she was telling you was real? Or are you totally disconnected from your intuition, never having felt, seen, or heard her guidance?

- What are your beliefs about intuition? Do you believe logic is more important than intuition, or the other way around? Or do your beliefs lie somewhere in between?

- What are some specific instances in which you trusted your intuition? What were the outcomes? Why did you choose to listen?

- What are some specific instances in which you ignored your intuition? What were the outcomes? Why did you ignore or doubt it? What would have been different if you had listened?

- In what way does your intuition tend to communicate with you? Do you just "know" things? Feel them in your body? Hear sounds or voices? See images, either while awake or asleep? What do you notice about yourself — physically, mentally, emotionally — when you are acting according to your intuition?

Why Don't We Listen?

While there may be many reasons why women ignore their intuition and instead choose logic, obligation, and fear, there is no *good* reason to stuff this magical ally into the closet. We owe it to ourselves, and to all the women who follow in our footsteps, to bring intuition — truly a girl's best friend — out in the open and into the conversation.

One of intuition's biggest nemeses is our society. Although all men and women are born with an inner knowing, we are conditioned to shut it off and embrace societal norms and rational thinking. No matter that intuition has guided women for centuries to do everything from raise a child to save a village, Western society has taught us to accept only the visible, the tangible, instead of what we know, sense, and feel inside. Intuition has not been woven into our Western way of life — it's not a topic for the dinner table, mainstream media, or mother-daughter chats. In a belief system in which facts are king and intuition is treated like a jester, intuition gets dismissed.

This inevitably leads us to make decisions based on obligation — another enemy of intuition. Regardless of what we may feel is the best course of action, when a sense of obligation is running the show, we listen to the "shoulds" over everything else. I should do this. I should do that. If I don't do this, then that person will be angry, upset, and so on. I cringe to think about how many women live their lives according to the shoulds instead of their inner guiding voice. Our intuition doesn't give a damn about the shoulds; she *always* makes finding what's best for us her number one priority. Thank goodness! Contrary to what many of us have been brainwashed to believe, this doesn't make her, or us, selfish. It makes her our ally on our mission to choose ME before WE, one who guides us to the actions that lead to loving and being ME.

The last, and possibly most destructive, force countering

intuition that I will mention is fear. Nothing makes us less likely to follow our intuition, and does more damage to our lives, than this four-letter word. The sad truth is that we are far more likely to make decisions based on fear than on our inner knowing. Part of the problem is that, as unskilled listeners, we often confuse intuition's voice with fear's negative bantering. And when fear is in control, boy, can we make a mess of our lives. If we are fortunate, we learn to distinguish between the two voices and, over time, learn to trust intuition more than the nasty four-letter word.

In the past, I was an expert at steamrolling right over my intuition whenever I didn't like what she had to say. At the time, I had no idea that I even had intuition, but I was aware I had feelings, thoughts, and dreams that seemed to be trying to get my attention. Looking back with a full understanding of, and trust in, my intuition, I can see that, in the months before my engagement ended, my inner guide was shouting, "This relationship is WRONG!" She persistently showed me that I actually wanted a life entirely different from the one I was living. But I wasn't listening. One way she tried to get my attention was in the form of dreams, both when I was awake and when I was asleep. These dreams were filled with snapshots of me and another man, in a different bed, living in a house in a big city, both of us feeling happy and free. I could see this person, even feel him, and I knew deep down that these dreams were reflections of my desire to be in a fulfilling relationship with a true partner, living the life *I* really wanted.

But the honesty of these visions was way too much to handle. Acknowledging them would have required me to face the fact that I was seriously unhappy with my fiancé, and I wasn't willing to do this, especially not based on some random "hallucinations." Now I know that the movies playing in my head were my intuition trying desperately to show me that what I wanted was possible. Unskilled as I was in understanding intuition, instead of heeding the message,

I rationalized the weird dreams and focused on my goal of ratifying an unhappy fifteen-year relationship with a marriage. That was *my* vision, intuition be damned. Had I listened to my best friend, I could have avoided the pain of having a brick wall topple on me. I could have created a much better, less dramatic and painful ending.

❤ ME Reflections ❤

What do you want copiloting your life — fear, society, logic, and the shoulds, or your intuition? You get to decide what influences your decisions and, ultimately, creates your life. Most of us don't realize we have such an important decision to make until we shut off our autopilot and become self-aware. You already made the choice to turn off your autopilot. Now it's time to look at the various forces vying to become your copilot, and consciously decide which one you want.

- What currently has the most influence on your decisions, beliefs, and relationships: your fear, societal norms, logical thought, the shoulds, or intuition? Rank them in order from most influence to least influence. Then, in your own words, describe how each one specifically influences you.
- How good are you at telling the difference between these influences? Make a list of at least ten decisions you've made during your life, decisions both big and small, both smart and not-so-smart. Which ones were responses to fear? Societal pressure? Logic? Obligation? An inner knowing? How did the outcomes differ?
- What do you believe about *intuition*? About *logic*? About *obligation*? What are your friends' opinions? What are your family's attitudes? How do these beliefs, opinions, and attitudes benefit you? How do they limit you? Which ones do you want to keep, and which do you want to throw in the trash?

- Which of these influences — intuition, fear, society, logic, or obligation — do you want copiloting your life?

The good news is that each of us has ultimate control over what we let guide our life — intuition, fear, society, logic, or obligation. Intuition is without a doubt the best guide a woman could ever have. Coupled with our intelligence, compassion, and love of life, intuition can help us create the life we want to live every day. But be aware that, although learning how to distinguish between your intuition and negative forces is possible, it's not easy.

Increasing Your Intuitive Power

So where should a girl start if she wants to become a pro at listening to her intuition? First, she must learn to listen each time intuition speaks. Then it becomes a matter of learning to trust what she feels and knows, even when she can't explain it rationally. Increasing one's intuitive power takes time and practice — the more you listen, the more you trust, and vice versa. The good news is, it can be a lot of fun.

Step 1. Learn to Listen When Intuition Speaks

No matter how weak your current connection to your intuition may be, no matter how often you ignored or doubted her in the past, she's still here for you 100 percent! We're all born with intuition — yes, ALL of us — and our ability to tap into her is never lost. It may wane, but we can always reestablish or increase the flow.

As a first step, you must be willing to believe that your inner sense is real. Embrace the possibility that something other than logic, fear, and obligation can guide you. I'm not suggesting that you ditch logic, but I am asking you to ditch your skepticism and be open to what your intuitive sense says. Listen when it speaks, and don't launch into a rational debate with yourself. A little initial skepticism may be natural when trying something new, but at some point you have to let go of your doubt and start trusting the truth you hear or sense inside.

Intuition gets her feelings hurt when we constantly doubt her wisdom, and over time, if we continue to ignore her, the other influences (which don't have our best interests at heart) will become louder and her voice will become harder to hear. Our intuition is like a muscle that we need to continue to build or else she atrophies. And, the more we use her, the stronger she gets. Don't ignore your intuition when she gives guidance that you don't like or that you can't explain with logic. That's usually when you need her most, and when destructive forces are just waiting to take control. Don't be afraid of what your intuition tells you. Be concerned about what you choose to ignore. Ignoring our intuition is what gets us into trouble.

Listening requires slowing down. You cannot hear the voice of intuition when you're running a million miles an hour or have been overtaken by fear. When your intuition reaches out to you, or when you can't figure out what she's saying, stop! When that feeling in the pit of your stomach or middle of your chest announces itself, stop, get really present with yourself (and quiet), and ask, "What is my intuition trying to tell me?" When the wise voice in your head (not the self-doubting, anxious one) starts talking, take heed. When you just know something is true, even when you have nothing logical to back it up, listen and act anyway. Notice what happens.

Listening means asking for advice and then waiting for a response. We are so well trained to jump into action that we don't give our intuition a chance to get a word in edgewise. Let her speak *before* you act. Practice connecting to your intuition throughout the day as you make everyday decisions. Simply close your eyes, take a deep breath, and ask for her opinion. Then listen for a physical,

auditory, or visual response, whichever form your intuition tends
to take.

Another way to build up your intuition muscle is to call on it
when you're feeling anxious or unsure about a situation, person,
or choice. When we react with fear or make statements like "The
reality is . . . ," or "It's just not practical . . . ," or "C'mon, be real-
istic," we are usually disconnected from our intuition. One thing
you can do to better connect with your intuition is to become quiet
and to connect with your body. This immediately calms and cen-
ters you and lets you avoid the spinning, scattered feeling that fear
causes. When we're spinning, we become ungrounded and tend
to make reactive, defensive choices. I experience this as what I call
"girl on overwhelm." In this state, we feel as if every bit of energy
that we have exists in our brain only. We cannot hear our intuition
when we're occupying the place that many spiritual teachers call
the "monkey mind." Intuition requires calm, and this means getting out of our head and into our entire body.

Exercise: GET INTO YOUR BODY

There are lots of ways to get into your body and out of the
spin. One way is to close your eyes and get grounded. This
means putting your feet on the ground and moving your
toes until you can feel your connection to the earth. You
may have to take your shoes and socks off and stand in your
bare feet so your flesh can feel the ground. Once you have the
connection, send the energy from your feet up your legs,
torso, and arms, and then up to your neck and head. For some
people, starting with the head and sending the energy from
the top of the body down to the feet is easier. When I do go
from top down, I like to imagine warm silver rain washing

down me from head to toe, clearing away everything, so that all that's left is total peace. Either direction works. Just make sure to breathe deeply, completely sensing your breath as it moves in and out of your body. Keep going until you feel calm and centered, and from this place talk to your intuition.

Give these techniques a try now — c'mon, it'll be fun! And then, when difficult situations or emotions surface, try them out again. Practice finding calm and, from that place, call your intuition forth. Practice really does make perfect when it comes to knowing and listening to your intuition, and it's the only way you'll learn to trust her.

Step 2. Learn to Trust Your Intuition

For skeptics, this can be the hardest step of all. But without trust in your intuition, you can't benefit from her sage counsel. A few women learn early on to take intuition at face value and have little problem believing in her and taking her guidance. Most continue to doubt her existence and sometimes just flat out ignore her. Some of us eventually wise up, once we have enough bumps and bruises from bad decisions, and finally realize that we need to get out of our heads and fears and into our hearts and spirits — the home of intuition.

The only way to truly learn to trust your intuition is to play with her in everyday life. The more positive results we gain from listening, the more we trust. I recommend that you start by making small choices based on this inner knowing. Don't give away the whole checkbook on day one. As amateurs, we need to build strong connections with our intuition from the ground up, making our connection with intuition stronger than our response to fear and our dependence on logic, which have been growing strong throughout our entire lives. It takes practice to distinguish between her positive influence and the negative forces lurking in the darkness.

Every day, just "notice." Increase your awareness of your inner sense. Start to distinguish between your responses to fear, to the shoulds, to logic, and to intuition. Consciously choose which one you give credence to. Notice what happens when you accept intuition's guidance. Notice what happens when you don't.

Getting to know and trust your intuition is a process that can change your life, as well as be a lot of fun! The logical mind, while certainly important, is far less creative. When we let go and receive the wisdom of our inner guide, so much more becomes possible. Using both our intuition and our intellect, we can live with two powerful forces on our side.

❤ ME Reflections ❤

What would your friends say if you asked, "Am I a skeptical person? Do I get stuck in my head a lot? How often do I do something because it's the 'right' thing to do or the 'logical' or 'practical' choice?" If you don't know, ask them. Think about their answers, and be honest with yourself about how you might be pushing intuition away. Here are a few questions to consider in order to uncover how doubt or guilt is affecting the power of your intuition.

- How skeptical are you in general? When examining a situation, do you tend to start with what could go wrong or with what is possible? How does your skepticism affect your ability to trust your intuition?
- What kind of decision maker are you? Do you put logic above all else, needing lots of evidence to make a choice, or do you tend to make decisions based on gut feelings or a combination of both? If you rely heavily on logic, when

has logic stopped you from listening to and trusting your intuition? What was the effect? What do you believe logic can give you that intuition can't? What would be different if you were to recognize that intuition has powers that logic doesn't? How likely are you to make choices out of a sense of obligation? Are you constantly laden with guilt about how your actions affect others, or do you feel free to take the action that feels best, regardless of other people's expectations or demands? When have you pushed your own feelings aside to do what's "right" according to someone else's standards? What has that cost you?

- What must you start or stop believing in, or doing, if you want to have more access to your intuition?

So What's It Going to Be?

The choice is yours: learn to trust yourself — to the best of your ability — by deepening your connection with your intuition, or continue holding on to skepticism, fear, and obligation. Which do you choose? I'm not asking you to be perfect, or to throw your rational self out the window. I am asking you to make a vow to yourself to listen to and trust your intuition.

☺ VOW TO LISTEN TO MY INTUITION ☺

I commit to listening to my intuition, to believing that she is real, and to learning to trust her guidance more and more every day.

Of course, as you did with the earlier vows, use your own words. And remember that all this promise, like any promise, takes is willingness — in this case a willingness to listen to your intuition and act on what it tells you. Learning to rely on intuition can only bring more good into your life. As you open up to her wisdom, your life will expand with new possibilities. Give yourself permission to play with your intuition, increasing her presence and power in your life and sending your fear running. Remember to be patient as you learn to live by intuition instead of fear, skepticism, and a sense of obligation. Trusting her to be a reliable copilot takes time, just as it does to build trust in a friendship.

Delving Deeper
CHOOSING YOUR COPILOT

Hundreds of books have explored fear in great detail, and rightfully so, as it keeps most of us living way beneath our potential. While I'm not going to launch into a dissertation on fear here, we are going to delve deeper into the fears that drive your decisions about life and relationships. Because fear is such a despicable and nefarious foe of intuition, I'd do you an injustice if we didn't. If you hope to trust yourself and use your intuition as the helpful tool that it is, you have to be aware of, and honest about, your fears. Then you can make conscious choices. Fear will try to hijack your decision making every time, so it's best to know where your fear is hiding.

Something that has helped me become aware of my fears is to think of them as gremlins who want to control my every thought and action. Gremlins speak with a voice, as does intuition, but their words fill us with doubt, tear down our self-esteem, make us second-guess ourselves, and keep us picking the safe and easy route. I envision my gremlins as nasty little green creatures with sharp fangs. Your gremlins may look different, but whatever form yours take, their work is the same: they dig into your psyche with thoughts that bring you down and elicit primal fear. Do any comments in the following list sound familiar to you?

Gremlin Banter

You will never succeed, so why even try?

Take what you have, and be happy.

You're not good enough.

No one will ever love you for who you really are.

Who are you to think yourself so special?

All the good men are taken.

You don't deserve better than this.

You're getting older, so you'd better hurry up and find someone.

He's going to leave you anyway, so you're better off leaving him first.

Oh, you shouldn't have said that! Now you look like a big idiot or a needy basket case.

I'll bet you have other comments you could add to this list. Fear has many ways to stomp on your intuition. But gremlins stay powerful only as long as we refuse to confront them face-to-face. So let's get them out into the light. Yes, you're going to go inside and call them forth!

Exercise: CONFRONTING YOUR GREMLINS
Step 1. Recall

Close your eyes and think about times in life when you've doubted yourself or changed course midstream because of fear. Remember how afraid you felt to take a risk, to put yourself out there, to do what you knew deep down would make you happy. Remember instances when you gave up or made a choice out of comfort. Hear those nagging voices listing your insecurities? "You're not good enough." "What you think doesn't matter." "You can't do it." Feel the force of your gremlins pulling you back. Really let yourself recall the negative words these gremlins used to breed doubt and fear inside you.

Step 2. Discover the Digs

Get a pencil and paper and list all the statements these gremlins have used against you. What exactly did the gremlins say to you? Write the statements in their voices, using simple words with simple sentence structure, language a five-year-old can understand: "You can't do it." "They'll laugh at you." "No one likes you." "He doesn't really love you." Gremlins talk directly to our inner child when they taunt us, which is how they stay so effective. They know that our little kid hasn't a chance against their ferocity.

When you think your list is complete, keep going. There will be a few more digs stuck inside. Push yourself to remember all of the overwhelming doubts that have stopped you in the past.

Step 3. Meet Your Group of Gremlins

Now it's time to bring the gremlins out and deal with them on *your* terms. Your goal is to personify one unique gremlin for each negative thought. As the gremlins become more real to you, you can address and deal with them directly, taking them out of the shadows where they normally stay as they poke at your deepest fears. One by one, read each "dig" you captured and envision what kind of gremlin is spewing these awful words. Give each nasty creature a name, face, and body. Write their names next to the statements, draw images, do whatever helps bring them to life. The end product? A completely exposed group of self-destructive beliefs and emotions. Once they're out in the light, you have all the power!

Step 4. Be Aware

Proceed in your life with this heightened awareness. When a gremlin appears, speak directly to it and let it know it is NOT in charge. Some gremlins may remain in the deepest regions of your psyche. If so, you're engaged in a power struggle with them — but remember, if they are strong, you are stronger. They are *your* gremlins, and with patience and effort you can overpower them. Sometimes this requires speaking to them; other times they can be tamed with pure love. Don't be afraid to talk to them. Invite them to have a conversation, or even embrace your gremlins in a full body hug. You'll be surprised at the power of calmness and unconditional love. I can attest to how well love works to transform gremlins — it's much more effective than trying to kill or suffocate them. I've hugged many a nasty, loud gremlin until it turned into a loving puppy dog! As with anything that seems scary, when you get up close and see it with your heart, your fear just melts away.

CHAPTER *Five*

Honoring ME

Who Said Settling for Less and Sacrificing Are Mandatory?

HOW TO SAY NO! TO SETTLING FOR LESS AND YES! TO YOURSELF

We accept, almost as law, that relationships require us to make sacrifices and to settle for less than we want. Women settle for too little all the time — for the good-enough partner, for the it's-not-so-bad job, for lives that generally fall short of our dreams. We sacrifice our goals, needs, wants, happiness — even our health — daily. Society supports it. We buy into it. We convince ourselves that what we have is enough when, in reality, our spirits are practically dying for more. Instead of responding to what our souls scream for, we tell ourselves, "Who am *I* to ask for anything more?" But the critical question is, who are you *not* to expect and believe there is more?

We never *have* to settle for less; we *choose* to. We take an unhealthy and twisted pride in sacrificing our needs for the sake of others, tying our sense of self-worth to how much we give. It becomes impossible for us to imagine that *taking care of ME first actually allows us to love others more and do more for them.* We choose to believe that there is never enough of what we want, worry that time will run out before we find it, or that someone else will take *our* man, job, whatever, if we don't get there first — as if there were a limited supply. Always in a hurry or living in a state of lack, we sell ourselves short, settling for "good enough." And then, once we have the "good enough," we hold on to it for dear life. To consider a different possibility would be crazy.

So I say, let's get crazy and consider an entirely new alternative, because the truth is, settling and sacrifice suck. There is another, much better, option. We can choose to honor ourselves, expect more, and believe in possibility, every day. What would life be like if every decision you made was based on honoring your needs and feelings without guilt? What if your wants and dreams were your reality? What if settling was no longer part of your guidelines for life?

Like a lot of the fixes we get ourselves into, settling for less stems from adopting beliefs and ideals that limit us. We come to accept, without question, that "this is just how things are." If you've learned anything over the past few chapters, I hope it's that, despite "how things are," reality is what we make it. Knowing, loving, trusting, and being honest with ourselves constitute a solid foundation on which to create the life and relationships we want. Without an unshakable commitment to honor ourselves, to never settle for less than we want, we will continue to sacrifice our needs and bend our commitments to self. Let's examine some of the reasons why, and some of the ways how, we settle in our relationships. Take notice of what's true for you.

The Belief That There's Not Enough

For some reason, when it comes to men, we women choose to believe that, as time ticks away, there are fewer and fewer guys available. We tell ourselves "My Mr. Right has already been snapped up, so how about I take Mr. Pretty Good?" or "I better stay with Mr. Okay, because having something is better than having nothing." Many a woman has walked down the aisle or avoided heading to divorce court as a result of this demented logic. I know. I was one of them.

What about you? Have you ever been in a relationship in which you were unhappy but scared that, if you left, you'd never find someone else to love you? Or felt that you were never going to find your soul mate, while every woman around you seemed to be hitting the soul-mate jackpot? Or put immense pressure on yourself and settled for good enough because "the clock was ticking"? Me? Guilty of all three.

One of the more ridiculous beliefs I had while on autopilot, one that I can laugh at now, seemed undeniable at the time: "Only two men (my fiancé and a previous boyfriend) will ever really love me." I was convinced that, if one of these two guys was not my soul mate, then I'd be alone forever, and being alone was a fate worse than death. So I made the only choice I thought I had. Ex-boyfriend? Taken and off the market. Fiancé? Not the best fit, but the only apparent option, so I told myself I'd better stick with him. Settling for less cost me at least ten years in an unhappy relationship.

As we get older it's probable, and maybe even certain, that a smaller number of single men exist. So what? The Truth, with a capital *T*, is that there are enough good men to go around. If we are having trouble finding one, let's stop blaming the numbers and start looking at ourselves. Maybe being single is the best thing for us right now. Maybe Mr. Right hasn't come along yet because *our* actions and beliefs are repelling the exact thing we're trying to attract. Whatever the reason, time alone is often a blessing and a big part of personal discovery. Why can't we just be okay with being on our own? Why do we get so hung up on being alone,

CHOOSING **ME** *before* **WE**

instead of embracing our solo period and learning what it has to teach us? And besides, while there may be many reasons why a man isn't in the picture, it's not because there aren't enough good men on the planet to choose from.

Possibility: There Is Enough for All

Contrary to popular belief, the world is not like one big pie with a fixed number of pieces, so that, once those slices are taken, there is no more pie left. And just because one person gets a bigger slice than we have now doesn't mean we can't have as much or more. When someone else receives good fortune, our own possibilities for good fortune don't diminish. Our potential for happiness, joy, and wealth is limited only by *our* thoughts and actions, not by what anyone else receives. If we believe we'll never have enough, or if we fear losing what we have, the state of our lives reflects these worries. Feelings and thoughts of lack = more lack = a life full of lack. I don't know about you, but I'm not so interested in lugging around a big sack of lack!

Somehow, many of us forget, or perhaps never learn, the liberating truth that we can always create more. I certainly never got this point until I began to meet self-aware people living lives that were successful *and* happy in all aspects. From watching them and listening to their stories, I learned that we all have access to what we want, if we are willing to

- give up our belief in scarcity, and start believing that anything is possible;
- stop worrying about losing what we have or not getting what we need, and trust that we will always have what we need to survive and thrive; and
- understand that how much someone else receives is irrelevant to what we can have, and know that we don't have to compete for resources or men.

Much has been written on the subject of limitlessness, which includes subjects like prosperity and the law of abundance. These are great ideas to study and implement in your own life — they've made a big difference in mine, that's for sure. On www.mebeforewe.com you can find a list of fantastic resources that will help you let go of the belief that "there isn't enough" and trade it in for the ability to trust, have faith, and surrender control. While becoming skilled at doing all three doesn't happen overnight, you don't have to be a yogi or the Dalai Lama to say no to settling for too little and yes to honoring yourself. You can make this commitment at any time, and it can change your life in a flash.

❤ ME Reflections ❤

- When have you settled for less or sacrificed yourself to stay in a relationship? What lies did you use to convince yourself that your choice was a good one? What did that choice cost you?
- What's in your "sack of lack"? What self-limiting beliefs about scarcity do you hold on to? What are you so worried about losing or not getting that you compromise your true desires? When do you feel like you need to compete with or take from others to get what you want?
- How often do you believe that anything is possible? When don't you, and what stops you from believing? When you don't, how does this drive you to settle for less?
- When is it easy for you to trust and have faith that everything will work out for the best? When is it hard? How does this faith affect your ability to create the relationships and life you want?

Some women might honestly say, "I will *never* settle for too little" or "I've never settled for too little." And this may be true. But most of us have settled for less than we wanted at one time or another. And we keep settling and making excuses until one day we say, "Enough!" and finally commit to ME in *all* parts of our life, especially in matters of the heart. This kind of commitment requires an unbreakable vow to honor one's self, which isn't always easy to keep. Over the course of life, even with our promise, settling can become an enticing option when we're plagued by worry and fear and our self-doubt kicks in hard. One of the best ways to prevent ourselves from giving in and settling for less is to become fully aware of our unhealthy motivations and the resulting situations.

Settling as a Result of Unhealthy Motivations

As single women, we tend to fret when our friends begin to marry, obsess when we think our biological clock is running out of time, and start believing that maybe something is wrong with ME. In relationships, we convince ourselves that our unhappiness is really our fault, or not that big a deal. We often become so focused on the goal of getting or staying married that we sell out our own hearts for a man. Some of us become totally driven by the desire to get a ring on our finger, a man who'll walk down the aisle, or simply a warm body in bed. Others of us spend so much time daydreaming about the life we *will* have — the wedding, the house, the family — that we make concessions regarding the man we are actually committing to today. When we're dishonest with ourselves about our motivations, and when we forget to love and honor ourselves, we settle for less — whether we know it or not. Unfortunately, most of us don't figure out we're settling until rather late in the game.

My messed-up motivations drove me into an engagement that never should have happened. I was like a racehorse, focused on one goal — winning the race. The race and my goal were clear — to be married and beat all my friends to the altar. After all, they'd been dating for way less time, and, in my mind, *their* relationships were clearly flawed! Admitting defeat was not an option. Not getting married was an inconceivable alternative.

So I did what any obsessed, focused woman would do: I pushed my fiancé to propose. I dictated the day, the ring, even the store from which the ring had to be purchased. And on Christmas morning, he got down on one knee and asked me to marry him. I accepted, even though I knew I was settling for less than I wanted. That fateful morning, I made a deal to sacrifice part of my soul for a diamond and the hope of what "could" be. Six months later, the marriage and life I had dreamed of ended before it started.

The lesson I learned the hard way was: *When we settle, we don't choose ME; we choose LACK*. We let our fears and the shoulds drive us to bad choices. Do any of the following statements sound familiar?

- It (getting married, having kids, moving in together, and so on) is the natural next step to take.
- He's just nervous. He'll feel better when we get married, have kids, move in together, or something else.
- Something is wrong with me if I don't get married. Better to be married than single.
- Half of what I want is better than none. It could be worse.
- Better the devil you know than the one you don't.
- What I want doesn't exist.
- He'll change eventually.
- There isn't anyone better out there.

So many of us push our relationships forward even when we know damn well that the person we're with isn't the right one. Whatever the reason — we're afraid to be alone, we desperately want to be married, we're determined to make it work — it all ends in settling for too little because our goal of being with a man becomes way more important than keeping a promise to ourselves.

Have you ever found yourself getting upset at the news that someone else is getting married? Or listened to a friend whine, in her best victim voice, "Why is it never me? Why am I still single?" I think it's time that we, as self-empowered women, knocked off the tears and the woe-is-me attitude and asked ourselves, "Why isn't my relationship progressing? Perhaps there's a really good reason — like the fact that it shouldn't! Maybe instead of wishing so hard that I were getting married, I should be honest about why I'm not. What is really motivating me?" Sometimes we are afraid of honesty. Shouldn't we be more concerned with wasting our precious lives?

I can still vividly remember the day one of my best friends got married. It was the only wedding I've attended in which I actually thought someone would stand up when the minister asked, "Can anyone here say why this man and this woman should not be married?" In that moment, I looked at my friends sitting in the pews, they looked at me, and we all glared at each other, thinking, "Do we say something? Do we stand up and scream, 'Don't do it!'?" In the end, none of us did, the couple got married, and six months later they were in the midst of a painful divorce. It was a case of unhealthy motivation. I'm not sure whether the bride was motivated more by the thought of having a husband (as if any nice guy would do), getting out of her parents' house and into her own (moving out on her own would have been easier), or the extravaganza of the wedding day.

How many women do you know who have spent most of their time imagining what the big day will be like, daydreaming about the fantasy of being married? I wish someone would burst their bubble *before* they walk down the aisle, and enlighten them to this reality: "A wedding is an event. Do yourself a favor and drop the fantasy and start thinking about the life you want to create with your partner beyond the wedding. Or better yet, decide what life you want to create for yourself. Or go even one step further: What if you decided to marry yourself first?" Now, that's something to dream into reality!

We're all motivated by something every time we make a decision. What sort of lives and relationships we create depends largely on where our drives come from. We've all made choices based on unhealthy motivations. The question is, can you afford to continue to do so? The answer is no, not if you want to honor the most important person in your life first: you.

❤ ME Reflections ❤

Use these questions to understand your own motivations — love, security, fear, a belief, a goal — for staying in a relationship, current or past, or your desire to find a partner, live with him, get married, and so on.

- Why do you want to be in a relationship? What are the motivating factors behind the reason(s)?
- When have your motivations led you to or kept you in a situation or relationship that wasn't good for you? What was driving you? What was healthy about your motivations? What was unhealthy?
- How have your relationships and life differed when you've been motivated by self-love and the desire to honor ME, rather than a sense of lack, fear, obligation, or outside influences?

Next, if you're not married or engaged, answer the following set of questions.

- Do you think you're "supposed to" be engaged or married by now, and do you wonder what's not working? Where does this belief come from? What action is it driving you to take?

- Why do you want to get married?
- If you never get married, how will you feel about yourself?
- When you're with your married friends, how do you feel about not being married or engaged? What judgments about yourself or your relationship do you have? How would you like to feel or think differently?
- If you have a partner answer the following: Do you think he'd better get into gear and propose? Have you considered why he hasn't? What's the truth behind why you're not engaged and moving toward marriage?

If you're in a relationship, answer the next set of questions about that relationship. If you're currently single, you can answer these questions with respect to past partners.

- What motivates you to stay in this relationship?
- Do you compare your relationship to others? If you do, why? What are you trying to justify or convince yourself of?
- Do you romanticize other people's relationships and believe their relationships are great because they're married or because they have something you don't? Tip: Stop creating stories and comparing. We never really know what other relationships are like. And these behaviors never lead to us feeling good.

If we're truthful about our motivations from the start, we can avoid tons of unnecessary misery. I encourage you to start checking in on what motivates your choices, feelings, and thoughts as a regular practice, simply by asking yourself the question, "What is motivating me to do, think, or feel this?" It's a good way to find truth and avoid settling for too little — especially when it comes to relationships.

The Reality of Settling: The Half Relationship

Settling for less in our relationships has the potential to create a lot of unhappy realities, one of which I've come to call the "half relationship." Simply put, it's a partnership that provides enough space for only a fraction of oneself to exist. In a half relationship, we share a house, finances, and perhaps even children with a man; however, the most *real* parts of who we are — things like our emotions, spirits, dreams, and unique self-expressions — are kicked to the curb or hidden away in the closet. Without room in the relationship for these essential parts of ourselves, we become desperate and lonely, and search out other avenues to express our seeking, intuitive, dynamic, sensitive, and evolving spirits.

We go hunting for people who can and will see us, people who will adore and appreciate us, people who we can connect with at deeper levels. And then we try piecing together these multiple relationships in an attempt to supplement our primary partnership. Unfortunately, most of us fail to get what we really seek, and we are left with more friends and obligations but not much more satisfaction. What we seek can *only* come from the connection with our lover. No matter how great they are or how many we have, substitutions don't quench our desire to have a complete partnership with the man we make love with and consider our life companion. This is not to say that we don't need relationships other than the one with our mate. Of course we do. Our friends, colleagues, families, and communities enhance our lives greatly. But no matter how much we receive from these others, when our partner can't "see" us, we lose out.

I can still recall a fight toward the end of my relationship with my ex-person that should have clued me in to the fact that something was very wrong. I was on autopilot at the time, firmly entrenched in my unhealthy motivations. For months, probably years, I'd been feeling so alone in our relationship, and I desperately wanted this man to really love *me*. I wanted him to see me for the unique and beautiful woman I was, but he was unwilling to do so, or perhaps incapable of it. On this particular morning, I stood at the edge of our bed and in total exasperation exclaimed, "You just don't see ME!" Those words rang out from the depths of my soul, and I stood there, my heart open wide, hoping the man I loved would finally get me, love *me* unconditionally. His reply was crushing. "Of course I see you. You're standing right in front of me," he said. He wasn't joking. He just didn't get it, or me for that matter. That conversation was one of the loneliest moments of my life.

I've witnessed so many women let their spirits wither away — even though their souls hungered deeply for more — just so they could stay in a relationship. This has to stop! Every woman deserves to be seen completely by a partner who can connect with *all* of her — but this can happen only if *we* won't accept less. Settling for the half relationship is like throwing a big piece of ourselves in the trash and, ultimately, saying to the world, "I am not worth more. My feelings are insignificant. I don't honor myself enough to insist on the love and friendship I want." It's like telling the most special parts of ourselves, "Hey, you are just going to have to deal with being lonely. Buck up and get used to a lifetime of yearning for real partnership."

Unfortunately, half relationships have been the norm for so long that most of us believe "that's just how it is." But our relationships are this way only because we *let* them be. My friend Tamara, for example, is a woman who's been committed to her own personal discovery and truth for more than fifteen years. However, she's also a woman who continues to settle for a half relationship in which her spirit lies dormant and unseen by the man she calls her husband. I share her story, the real-life tale of a woman consciously embracing self-awareness, to illustrate just how easy it is for a woman to find herself in a half relationship, even when she believes she's turned off autopilot.

Tamara's Story

Tamara lives a pretty typical American life, busily building a career, raising kids, and pursuing her other passions, writing, cooking, and Kabbalah. Cooking has been in her blood since she was a little girl. Passed down from generations and enhanced by her love of Italy, this passion feeds both her body and her soul. For as long as I have known her, she has sought a deeper connection to the world through both her formal Kabbalah practice and her adoration of cooking and writing.

Somewhere along the way, Tamara met and married Jack. On the surface, it appeared as if they had a lot in common. Jack loves to cook and write, and in fact he's a chef and a published author. In the beginning, their relationship seemed like it could be a fulfilling partnership. But as she got to know Jack better, Tamara learned that the guy she'd fallen in love with didn't believe in anything "spiritual." Awareness and personal discovery were not concepts in Jack's repertoire. She walked down the aisle anyway, banking on his eventually coming around because of her influence.

Several years and a few kids later, she is still waiting for Jack to wake up, to become aware that he needs to heal himself and grow. For more than a decade, he has continued to live on autopilot, stuck in his beliefs and ideals, while Tamara continues to grow spiritually and emotionally. As a result of Tamara's and Jack's widely different perspectives on life, large holes and vast valleys have formed in their relationship.

They share a house, three kids, and a retirement plan, but not much else. Jack isn't interested in finding or fixing himself, let alone admitting that he has a spirit. Tamara has tried tirelessly over the years to help Jack heal his wounds, to open up a dialogue about anything spiritual, but Jack doesn't want to understand or connect with her spirit. He's only interested in their physical and mental relationship. Their marriage lacks *deep* connection and communication, and it leaves Tamara constantly yearning for something she can't seem to find.

I imagine she stays in the relationship for many reasons — kids, money, even hope. Since Jack doesn't stop her from studying the Kabbalah, she continues to follow the path of spiritual and personal discovery on her own. Resigned to the fact that her spirit has no place in this relationship, she has separated her core values and ideals from her partnership. In effect, she treats her spirit like a removable Lego. But in reality, she can't just separate it from the rest of her self. Her spirit is embedded in every cell of her being. It is who she is. And so, she finds herself married but alone and unsupported by the man she sleeps next to every night. Her spirit survives only because of her solitary daily practice and her connection to other seekers, but the addition of children has made even that difficult. It's as if Tamara is being squeezed out of her own life. Yes, she did settle for too little, and she's the one who suffers the most.

All of You, Always

Tamara's story is not about the need for both partners to possess all the same beliefs. Quite the contrary, differing spiritual viewpoints can bring great depth to a relationship. Religion isn't the issue; our spirit is. Body, mind, *and* spirit — we are all three, and they cannot be separated. In our partnerships, unless both people are awake and healthy, we may end up checking our spirit at the door, particularly when we've created a half relationship.

Although body, mind, and spirit all inform how we live, it is our spirit that connects us to a reason for being, to a higher purpose, to the talents and passions that make us come alive. Our spirit influences how we dance with life and death. It functions as our center for joy, love, sadness, and hope. Our dreams live in our spirit, and our creativity emanates from it. In the end, it defines who we uniquely are as a person. If we can't share our spirit freely and fully with our partner, we are nothing more than an empty, soulless body and mind. With only body and mind we can still form a contract to "survive" — the house, kids, boat, double income, and 401(k) — but that's just a business contract, and frankly, it's not enough.

What if you didn't have to settle for the contract? What if you insisted that your partner value all of you — body, mind, *and* spirit? You can handle the physical and mental aspects of life without a man. Contrary to the fairy tales that still subtly affect many a woman's motivations, you don't need a man to take care of you — and in fact, no one but you really can. You, and every woman, are entitled to so much more than the contract. You deserve the deep connection of a whole partnership, where your spirit can soar, you can be seen fully, and you can be you. This is the kind of bond that can bring your life to new levels of ecstasy and fulfillment. Honor yourself enough to choose nothing less.

❤ ME Reflections ❤

Are you in, or have you ever been in, a half relationship? Think about the interactions you have or have had with a partner, and answer the following questions.

- Are there feelings, parts of your life, or topics that you don't share with your partner?
- Are there aspects of yourself that he just doesn't get, no matter how thorough the explanation?
- Does he dismiss what you have to say, or act like he just doesn't care?
- Would he rather turn on the TV or change the subject than have a meaningful conversation?
- Do you sometimes feel lonely, even when he's around?
- Do you wish you could connect with a deeper part of your partner, and are you unable to find the right words?
- Is there a lack of intimacy, emotional or physical, between the two of you?

If you answered "yes" to any of these questions, chances are you've been settling for a half relationship. Even if you answered "no" to all, I encourage you to reflect on the inquiries below, written to help you find the truth about the kind of connection you really have with your current partner or one you've had in the past. If you're not in a relationship right now, this exploration will still be valuable. Remember, we tend to repeat patterns until we become aware of them.

Answer the following questions in relation to your connection with your current or previous partner.

- Do you connect with each other beyond the mental and physical? How do you connect emotionally? Spiritually?
- How does he react when you talk about problems or your feelings? Will he talk them out? Does he take responsibility or play the blame game? Do you believe that you deserve a man who will communicate, especially during difficult times?
- Is *all of ME* present when you're with this man? Does he love you exactly as you are, or are there conditions? (A

partner should love *every* bit of you, even if he doesn't *like* every piece. If he continually points out how you are wrong or that you need to change, or tells you not to express your thoughts, ideas, or feelings, beware! Your spirit is likely being suppressed, even sacrificed, for the relationship.)

- Do you have moments of doubt about this man or question whether the relationship truly has space for all of you? What are those doubts? What are they trying to tell you? What are you afraid to hear?
- Can you say with honesty, "My man really gets me; he absolutely sees me"? How do you know?

If you are married or otherwise partnered, answer the following questions.

- Is your life more like that of a single woman? Do you find yourself going to events, pursuing activities, or looking for fun alone or with friends when you really want to be there with your partner (that is, beyond spending a healthy amount of time alone, do you feel as if you are always without him)? Are you happy even though he isn't there? If you tell yourself, "It doesn't matter that I do this alone," are you really being honest?
- Do you make excuses — he has to work, he's not sociable, it's a financial issue, he doesn't like your friends, and so on — when your partner is absent? If so, how does it feel to make excuses?
- Do you want a partner you can share life experiences with? If you don't have that partner, why don't you? What lies have you been telling yourself?

After surviving my own half relationship, I promised myself I'd never settle for the contract again. Since it was clear that my

spirit had been in the closet for way too long, I promised that in
the future I would choose only a man who would welcome all of
me with open arms. Honoring myself so completely allowed me
to create a relationship with a true partner, one who adores and
honors *all* of me. I see all of me, and so does he. Having existed
in both half and whole relationships, I understand why we settle,
and I know we don't have to. Honestly, I would prefer to have no
relationship than a half relationship, any day. I can provide all the
"contract" stuff myself. It's the emotional and spiritual support,
affection, and partnership that is priceless. What I want is a companion to experience and explore the full range of life with. *This*
feeds my spirit. Do you know what feeds yours? Are you willing
to insist that your spirit be nourished? Are you willing to ask for
and create a whole and fulfilling relationship?

Delving Deeper

MAKE THE CHOICE TO STOP SETTLING AND START HONORING ME

To stop responding to a sense of lack, and to stop settling for too
little, you'll have to make the commitment to honor yourself.
You must start to expect more. You've got to begin believing that
what you want is possible. By now you know that, if you don't
believe in what you want or insist on it, you can't create it. No one
but you is going to give you the life you want. The question is, are
you ready to believe that you deserve it, willing to let yourself have
it, and ready to stand up and take it? If so, you're about ready to
take the vow to always, always, always honor the most important
person in your life first: you.

Before taking this vow, ask yourself a few questions that will
help you clarify what you want. Use your answers to write your
vow to honor ME. The wording of the vow included here can help
you get started.

Pre-vow Inquiries

- In your life and relationships, what do you choose to stop settling for?
- In your life and relationships, what do you choose to believe you deserve?
- What do you insist on receiving from your partner? From all people in your life?
- What are *you* willing to give?

⬯ VOW TO HONOR ME ⬯

I commit *right now* to no longer settling for less, to throwing out my sack of lack, to being impeccably honest about my motivations, and to choosing to live a life of possibility and abundance while deeply and truly honoring the beautiful woman I am.

Bonus: Honoring ME Mantra

In honor of your commitment, I offer you the following affirmation, a mantra you can use to create a life and relationship that honors you. Say this affirmation daily, weekly, hourly — once, fifty times, a hundred times — whatever it takes to persuade yourself to stop settling for too little. This affirmation won't solve all your problems, but it will help you shift your beliefs and make this statement a reality:

I deserve to have everything I need and want in a partner and in my relationship. When I am true to myself, it's possible to have it all.

PART *Two*

HE

CHAPTER Six

Choosing Your Core Four

GET THE MAN YOU WANT BY FIRST GETTING CLEAR ON WHAT YOU REALLY WANT

*W*hether she's in a relationship or single, every woman needs to know what she wants in a man, regardless of who is or isn't currently sleeping in her bed. How can we expect our partners to be the men we want them to be if we have no clue about what we desire from a partner, or why we even want one in the first place? How can we be upset that we haven't attracted our soul mate if we don't know what's *really* important to us? We can't. By now you know that every relationship starts with ME. What you need to understand next is that, unless you're really clear about what you want in a HE, you're not likely to get it.

Among other things, this requires you to stop making, revising, comparing, and holding on to any variety of "man list" you've ever fabricated. This means no exhaustive inventories of qualities that a man needs to have in order to be "the one." No litanies of standards he must measure up to: Does he dress and look right? Will my parents like him? What will my friends think? What kind of future does he have? My goodness, who could pass an inquisition like this or possess the fifteen or twenty traits (many of them superficial) that we may have committed to memory? We might as well shove the poor guy into a computer and watch the reject sign flash on screen.

I shudder to think how many of us have been guilty of meeting a guy and, within the course of a few dates (if even that many), beginning to measure him against our standards and checklists. How many of us have ended a relationship because his "packaging" — looks, job, background, future, friends — was all wrong, even though he made us smile from head to toe? How many of us let our friends or families deter us from following the truth in our own hearts?

Even if you've never made a man list in your life, you're not off the hook! Having no clarity about what you want is just as bad as having a lengthy list of requirements. If we don't give deliberate and heart-centered thought to what we want, how can we complain about what we do have, or wonder why HE hasn't shown up yet? It's unacceptable to answer the questions "What are you looking for in a partner?" and "What's important to you about a man?" with an emotionless response like "I want a good man who is funny, smart, handsome, and financially stable." Ugh! Make me celibate now! What an unimpassioned way of determining the kind of guy we want to live with for the rest of our lives. Unfortunately, it's exactly the way many of us approach finding the partner of our dreams. No wonder we're so often dissatisfied.

The good news is, this is all about to change. When you finish this chapter, you'll have a crystal-clear understanding in your soul of why you want a partner, and you'll be able to articulate with passionate lucidity who that man is. If you're in a relationship, you'll be able to locate the gaps between what you have and what you want so you can actually do something about them beyond just complaining. If you're single, you will crank up the power of intention to draw this person to you. Allow me to introduce you to the magic of the "Core Four."

The Core Four

Based on one fact — what you focus on, you will attract — the Core Four is the power of intention put to work to attract the partner you want. In its simplest form, the Core Four works like this: *Focus* and *express* the four core *essences* that your heart and spirit — not your mind, ego, or fear — want in a partner, and you will attract what you desire.

Focus is a critical ingredient for powerful intentions. Sometimes women ask me, "Why four; why not five or six?" I've found four to be the perfect number because it allows for both specificity and enough space to express what we want. Concentrating on four demands clarity and keeps us from defaulting to the list of bulletpoints. While the women and men I've shared this with have occasionally begged for five or six, I've told them, "Save your breath." It is the Core *Four*. If you try to focus on too much, the power of your intentions will dissipate and you'll get mediocre results at best.

Energy is another key component of powerful intentions. If your intentions have little meaning to you, or if they come from an unhealthy place, they'll fall flat and so will the outcome. Identifying four specific essences that matter to us, and committing to finding a man who has them, is like building a giant man magnet. Clarity and the ability to emotionally express an *essence* — rather than a trait, attribute, or characteristic — is critical to manifesting success. The universe responds to the energy created by feelings — passion, love, curiosity, pain, joy. When considering the partner we want to attract, we can't be in our heads thinking about him; we need to be in our hearts, feeling the answers to questions like:

"Who is this man at his core? What does he stand for? What does he bring to the world just because of who *he* is?" We must be able to feel his spirit and yearn to know his soul, not his résumé. Discovering your Core Four is not like creating a PowerPoint presentation. The process of uncovering the man you want in your life should feel like creating a vivid, vibrant, and lifelike painting that stirs your emotions and lights your spirit up like a firefly.

Of course, as with anything of value, setting intentions powerful enough to manifest someone requires effort and consideration and a broadening of your self-awareness. Your Core Four won't roll immediately off your tongue like a shortened man list or a dispassionate string of bullet points. No, setting your intention to come up with a Core Four that actually works requires thought, openness, honesty, and commitment to the following four steps, which we will go through together in detail.

Four Steps to Attracting Your Core Four

1. Clear away any misguided ideals or beliefs standing in your way of intention-setting and manifesting.
2. Discover what you really want in a partner and why you desire one at all.
3. Create your own Core Four.
4. Commit to attracting the partner you want, whether you currently have one or not.

Oh yeah, one last thing... let's do this with a sense of discovery and fun. Think of it as your very own Core Four adventure, firmly grounded in what's ultimately most important — the love you have for yourself.

Step 1. The Clearing Process

Let's clear away anything that is going to get in the way of creating your Core Four. In this clearing process, first we'll make sure you are fully aware of the rules of intention setting, including the Core Four caveats. While attracting what we want is as simple as focus + energy + action, it's also as complicated as all the illusions and fears we cling to and that, quite frankly, get in our way. Second, we will clear away all previous or current men who are or have been in your life. While I know you understand that every relationship starts with you, it's been my experience that, when asked the question "What do you want in a partner?" many of us use our current or previous partners as models, especially if we don't want to admit that our current mate is not what we want, or if we believe that the one who got away should have been the keeper.

So, first things first. Let's dig into the three areas you'd best bone up on before setting out to create your Core Four: the fine print of intention setting, the packaging caveat, and the timing caveat.

Intention Setting: The Fine Print

I don't know many people who wouldn't want to benefit from the power of intention: *What you focus on, you create.* Who doesn't want to actualize their true desires simply by focusing on them? *Want* is not the problem. It's our attachment to instant gratification, material satisfaction, doubt, and fear that seem to render intention powerless. Following is some of the "fine print," or subtle intricacies, of working with intentions. Manifesting is a topic that people study for years. Many have become masterful at manifesting in many areas of their lives. For the purposes of this book, we are focused on attracting the partner you want, using the intentional power of the Core Four. If you're interested in becoming masterful at manifesting other desires, I've listed several resources on my website (see www.mebeforewe.com).

MAINTAIN YOUR INTEGRITY. The *soulless pursuit* of material objects and shallow aspirations is a crappy way to use the power of intention. All you usually get anyway is a superficial package that ultimately doesn't make you happy. Be honest about your motivations and where they come from. Let yourself be motivated only by desires centered in your heart and spirit. Stay away from intentions based on fear, the ego, and the shoulds.

STAY COMMITTED. Constantly wavering or changing your mind is like making the universe seasick. Be willing to stand firm and say, "Yes, this is what I want." Then take the actions required to get it. This doesn't mean your intentions are written in stone — life changes everyday. But there is no room to be wishy-washy. Either claim your desires or stop whining that you're unhappy.

LISTEN AND RECEIVE. Ignoring or manipulating the messages the universe sends, in whatever form it chooses, is a poor idea and one I highly discourage. Be fully open, aware, and unattached to what comes once you set an intention. Be willing to receive *all* of it. Sometimes when our desires come true, this brings so much love or joy to us that an overload occurs. You may be required to expand what I call your "happiness quotient," how much joy you allow in, or your "love quotient," how much love you can receive from another.

BELIEVE. Once you let doubt or skepticism creep in, the power of intention is useless. Challenge yourself to remain open to possibility and avoid negativity. Don't let your mind override your spirit. Be practical and live with the sense of possibility at the same time. It's about balancing the two, not picking one or the other.

BE GRATEFUL. This is really important and often ignored. Be grateful for what you have *today*. Too often, we focus so intently on what we want that being thankful for what already exists is the last thing on our minds. If you find it difficult to be grateful, challenge yourself once a day to say out loud what in your life you appreciate — you'll be amazed at how blessed your life already is.

The Packaging Caveat

Although most of us try, we cannot control the package our man comes in — how he looks or dresses, what he does (or doesn't do) for a living, where he resides, or how much money he has. To manifest the man you want, you have to surrender control of his packaging. He may be bald, short, tall, overweight, or obsessed with the color orange. He may have grown up living in a cardboard box, may be studying to be a florist, may have twelve toes, five cats, or whatever. Let your preconceived notions of all external qualities and measures go — or you will limit what you get.

The Core Four requires you to articulate lucidly and with passion who he is in his essence, not his résumé, family background, or financial portfolio. While your ego and fear may relish and find comfort in the physical and material stuff, it's your heart and spirit that will lead you into deep and meaningful connections and partnership. A man's essence — the core of who he is, the parts that make up his soul — doesn't change. Everything else can, and often does, change or disappear with age, sickness, stress, or a turn of the stock market. Be clear about the difference. Be honest about your own motivations.

While most of us get the difference in our minds, when faced with the reality of a prospective partner, not many of us really want to stop putting all kinds of physical and material restrictions on what kind of guy we'll call a boyfriend or husband. In fact, we'll even use these packaging specifications to shoo great guys out of our lives and keep crappy men in. The reasons are endless and may be valid concerns, but more often than not they're a distraction from what is actually occurring.

Intention setting requires integrity, and this means being impeccably honest about where your desires *really* stem from. Does the idea of having a handsome, financially successful, responsible, and well-educated man actually address some hidden fear or self-limiting belief or insecurity of yours? Are you so fixated on the vision in your head that the man you choose must fit your *perfect* image? I've heard many packaging-related reasons for dismissing a potentially great guy, and I've definitely used some of them myself. Here are two of the most common ones I've come across. Read them and commit them to memory so you can avoid falling into the packaging mistake yourself.

1. THERE'S JUST SOMETHING ABOUT HIM THAT TURNS ME OFF. If it feels like kissing a dead battery when your lips touch, for goodness sake, jump ship. But if there is any chemistry at all, be aware that we often confuse fear of connection with lack of attraction. If something about him turns you off, say, a small chin, but his personality makes you tingle in a good way, try seeing his true beauty and get over yourself. Same thing with a belly bulge, wild nose hair, or a receding hairline. Get past the physical aspect you've become fixated on and challenge yourself to look more closely at what you're afraid of. Is it intimacy? Love? Friendship? Actually being happy? And when you find out what's really going on with you, take another look at this fellow. Does he still make you tingle inside? Does the relationship bring you happiness? If you answer "yes," then, while he'll still have a [insert your made-up hang-up here], chances are it won't be such a big deal.

2. HE'S NOT [INSERT EXPECTATION], HE DOESN'T HAVE [INSERT EXPECTATION], AND HE'S NEVER GOING TO BE [INSERT EXPECTATION]. While it is true that none of us want to date, let alone marry, a loser, what most women fail to realize is that their egos and ridiculous expectations drive great men away. We want the successful, fully self-realized product today. But truthfully, the men who *appear* to have it all on the outside are often missing the depth, soul, and sensitivities we actually want. We've created a habit of judging men by what they are *not*, and as a consequence we shove away many great, self-aware men committed to evolving

into their best selves. We also love to rate our mates and measure them against other men and our own standards. I wonder how many women would appreciate being judged according to their papers, like cocker spaniels at a dog show? It's time women realized that just because a guy doesn't have the right credentials, education, or pedigree doesn't mean he's not everything we could want, and more.

Honestly, many times our packaging hang-ups have everything to do with our own issues, not his. You wouldn't be the first woman to realize that her issue with the guy she's dating is actually the result of her deep-seated fears, ignorant perspectives, or out-of-whack attitude. If you find yourself judging a guy by his packaging — looks, financial status, background, material success, or any other external expression — make sure you understand where your problem with his packaging originates. For example, if you really like a guy but are concerned about his career ambitions, notice where your doubts come from. Do your feelings come from your heart, where you have a genuine desire for this man to improve his life for himself (for example, to improve his self-worth by going for the job he deserves)? Or do the feelings stem from your personal fears and poorly considered judgments (for example, his paycheck is not big enough to keep you in the lifestyle you want)? Of course we want to be with a man who believes in himself, but that's very different from kicking a guy to the curb because he doesn't fit our financial ideal. Be honest about *your* issue and where it stems from.

I've witnessed many women get rid of great guys because they couldn't get past their own hang-ups to see what the relationship had to offer them. Sometimes people come into our lives to help us grow. Healthy *relationships* often act as catalysts for personal change (which is not the same as fixing someone). There's a big difference between trying to change someone and creating a relationship in which each individual helps the other become a better person. In healthy partnerships, we can inspire and influence someone who wants to make change, explore new possibilities, and grow with us.

So if you have doubts about a guy, take a step back. Stay grounded in what's important to you (choosing ME before WE) *and* separate what's true from what's clouded by any unfair judgments, comparisons, and personal issues. You could find yourself with a guy who truly is growing, who regards you as a source of inspiration, and who'll be a source of inspiration for you too.

The man I now call my best friend and life mate showed up with no hair and the fashion flair of a college frat boy. This was my introduction to the lesson "Do not be attached to the packaging." His mostly bald, but cleanly shaved, head was something I quickly warmed to. His clothing was another matter. It nearly let me convince myself that this charismatic fellow who made my insides tingle was not the person for me. No matter that being near him made my heart flutter; the sight of him in that purple-and-orange flannel coat, which hid a ripped University of Illinois sweatshirt beneath it, made me cringe. The sight of him standing at my front door in his brown leather bomber jacket from 1992 made me want to slam the door and run. This may sound shallow, but in truth, this was my attempt to conjure up obstacles to getting what I truly wanted — love, companionship, a man who really got me. These were the thoughts of a woman who wasn't ready to trust a new relationship. They were my self-created barriers to experiencing joy.

Thankfully, I had smart friends who reminded me that most men didn't have a clue about fashion unless they had former girlfriends who'd already done the makeover, or were gay or metrosexuals. Also a blessing was the fact that I was in therapy and could explore my contributing insecurities and fears. As was the fact that I'd chosen a partner who had the inner qualities I found essential. One of my Core Four qualities for a man was the commitment to becoming and being the best person possible — a perpetual willingness to fully experience life, to try new things and believe in new possibilities.

Noah was willing to grow, and this allowed him (and me) to understand the root of his bad coats, holey socks, and rumpled polo shirts, which were really only symptoms of his not taking better care of himself on many levels. Beneath the clothing were more serious symptoms, like a job he disliked, a lack of ambition, and a less-than-stellar credit score. As I became able to separate my own issues from the symptoms he displayed, we were able to talk about what was really going on. In the process, Noah discovered that the way he felt inside about himself affected how he presented himself on the outside, that he didn't really love himself and, because of this, didn't believe he deserved to dream big or have nicer things. With my support and love (note: not attempts to fix him), Noah changed his relationship with himself and his belief about enjoying abundance and prosperity as reflected in his clothes, his career, and his plans for his future. He began taking better care of himself. Because he was open to growth, he learned to love himself in a more holistic way. He changed the packaging that I'd tried to make a deal breaker. Had he not chosen to shift, I know the relationship would have ended. Not because he wore holey socks and bad coats, but because he wasn't willing to grow as a person, and that was a must-have for me. Had I not kept my heart and mind focused on my Core Four and given us the time to grow together, I never would have discovered his desire to create a better life for himself. He had to find it at his own pace and I had to let him, just as I had to clear up my own issues.

The Timing Caveat

Like it or not, you also don't get to pick the timing of when you will collide with a great potential partner. Often, it happens when we least expect or want it, so you might as well surrender now to the fact that your mate's moment of arrival is not your choice. Sure, you can choose to push a good man out or never let him in, but he'll be delivered either way, regardless of whether you accept the package.

Our task is simple, although we may try to make it difficult: notice when he shows up, and go with it. Maybe his arrival is inconvenient because we have started a new job, travel a lot, or are experiencing one of a thousand other scenarios. Perhaps we're going through emotionally hard times and a relationship is the last thing on our mind. Maybe we're even dating someone else when a new guy shows up. We may tell ourselves, "No, he couldn't be 'the one.'" We lose in all scenarios where we try to control the timing.

We don't have all the information about what's happening to us, no matter how much we like to believe we do. There are elements much greater than ourselves at work, and life yields amazing synchronicity, if only we will get out of the way. Most of us have experienced at least one situation we didn't understand at the time, and that, in hindsight, gave us precisely what we needed. Looking for love is no different. Trust that when your Core Four show up in a man, this guy's worth a shot. This is not to suggest that you should leave your current man because some guy you have the hots for appears. Listen to your intuition. Stay aware and listen deep inside for what is true for you. Trust in divine timing and leave logic out of it.

The brain just gets in the way, at least in my experience. The timing excuse, fully backed by logic, was one I used to try to push Noah away. It was easy to attempt, because he walked into my life so soon after my engagement ended. It made sense to tell him to take a hike. I was processing a lifetime of emotions, fears, insecurities, and hurt feelings. And although I didn't know it at the time, I was also in the infancy of my personal awakening. I'd turned off autopilot, stopped plugging my holes, and was on my way to becoming self-aware and healthy.

If I'd remained adamant that "it was just too soon," I would have shoved him right out of my life. My brain said it made sense, but my heart said, "Let him stay!" My rational self rallied hard to build a case against him, but Noah had a way of bringing perspective into a situation. Two months into our dating relationship, I told him, "I'm just not ready for a relationship." I was so used to having a relationship that I didn't know there were other options. His ingenious and sincere reply was, "Who said anything about a relationship? We can just spend time getting to know each other and having fun." Well, that took the pressure off! Hang out and have a good time without expecting some big relationship? What a concept!

Those few words made all the difference. With the timing issue out of the way, I surrendered control and received some of the best surprises of my life — unconditional love, support, gentleness, kindness, unabashed laughter, friendship, and compassion. I had never met anyone like Noah before, because I had never given myself the chance. I had never loved myself enough to let in that kind of love.

Now that you understand the rules and caveats of intention setting and manifestation, you're ready for the second part of our preparation: clearing all previous and current men from your mind. Your objective is to wipe the slate clean of any existing thoughts about, attachments to, or feelings for any specific male figure. If you're currently in a relationship, you must create your Core Four without thinking about your partner, otherwise his characteristics will color your choices. So, for the rest of this chapter, consider yourself single. Feel the freedom in that! Even if you aren't in a relationship, there are likely some traces of an old partner still hanging out inside your mind and heart. Erase all thoughts about your ex-guys and liberate yourself from all past expectations and perceptions.

If you find it difficult to completely clear yourself of any current or previous man juju, I suggest trying the orange liquid technique. It's very simple, yet 100 percent effective. Here's how it works: Close your eyes, imagine this man, feel his presence, and then pour orange liquid all over him, from head to toe, erasing any sign of his existence. Orange liquid him *away*, gone.

With a clean slate in hand, and with the spirit of an adventurer about to discover gold, promise yourself one last thing: the necessary time to find your Core Four, to find whatever *you* need to honor yourself. Taking the time to know what you truly want from a partner, without being influenced by current and past men, is one of the most important things you will ever do. Treat it that way.

Step 2. *The Discovery Process*

Now it's time to get the intention engines started! First step? Get crystal clear on why you want a partner in the first place. There are lots of choices at our disposal — staying single, dating, hooking up, shacking up, long-term partnership, marriage. Shouldn't we have an unambiguous understanding of what we want and why? Remember, intentions require focus.

With this understanding taken care of, you'll be free to let yourself fly into the realms of imagination to create your Core Four. Without limitations or reference to an existing mate, you'll begin to conjure up who this man is at his core. And don't forget, even if you have a guy today, you're on this adventure as a single woman. Before you ever put pen to paper, it's imperative to unreservedly immerse yourself in the essence of this special being, to envision his spirit, heart, and soul. In addition to requiring focus, manifesting requires us to resonate with the energy of that which we want to attract. That means feeling who this man is, with every part of your being.

I Want a Man Why?

It's really as simple as answering two sets of questions, and as hard as your unwillingness to be honest. Considering that in previous chapters we've already gone through, at great length, why self-honesty is not optional, we'll assume that truth won't be an issue for you. In other words, you must answer these questions with integrity, keeping in mind that you don't *need* a partner. *Wanting* one, now that's different. Needing one signifies desperation. Wanting one signifies empowerment.

1. What are you looking for when it comes to a relationship? Do you want to date one guy or many guys? Do you want a short-term but serious relationship? Are you looking for a man you can eventually marry, or do you desire a long-term, live-in partner? Or maybe you want a guy to stay with for years, but the two of you will keep separate residences. Do you want a partner to have children with you, and does that mean you need to be married?

2. *Why* do you want a _____ [fill in the blank according to your answer to the previous questions]? This may seem like an obvious question, but it's really not. Challenge yourself to look deep into your motivations for desiring this particular kind of relationship. Ask yourself, "Why isn't another type of relationship, level of commitment, or so on, what I want? Why do I believe this kind of connection will give me what I'm looking for? What are my healthy motivations? Do I have unhealthy motivations

— for example, fear, obligation, illusions, or a desire to get external things I think I can't get on my own?"

Once you've answered these questions and gained a solid focus, you'll be ready to move to the next part of the discovery phase: imagining and feeling who this guy is at his core.

Feeling the Energy: Use Your Imagination

Imagination requires us to let go of logic and open up to the free feeling of possibility. You may find that this is a natural state for you, or you may find it a challenge to leave rational arguments and skeptical questions at the door. All I ask is that you give the following visualization a chance, trusting it to take you deeper into yourself, where all the answers lie. Give yourself permission to check your logic at the door for a few minutes, and let your spirit and imagination lead the way. We will come back to practicality later on in the Core Four adventure.

To begin, find a quiet place where you won't be disturbed or distracted by people, electronics, or anything else that might compete for your attention. Choose somewhere you can be with yourself: with your heart, thoughts, and dreams. A spot where you can breathe easily and travel inward without worrying about the outside world. This is a journey into you, where all the answers, desires, and possibilities live, where your Core Four reside.

Get comfortable. No need for pen and paper yet. All you need in this moment is to connect with yourself. Feel your body, hear your breath, sink into your senses, be completely present right now. Close your eyes and envision a soft and warm silver rain streaming gently and steadily down from the top of your head, across your forehead and face, and down your body, all the way to your toes. Imagine this silver rain washing away all the day's worries and any anxiety about attracting the partner you desire. Let this beautiful, calming water flow. When you feel absolutely present in the moment, let one big breath out and feel the sense of connection. See yourself as the beautiful, magnificent, and unique spirit that you are, smiling and happy, feeling totally whole and taken care of within yourself.

Now, visualize giving yourself a giant, wrapped present tied with a magnificent bright-colored bow. This gift is the permission to imagine, the freedom to fly through all the possibilities for the life you want to create, the partner you want to have, and the person you want to be. Believe you deserve it. Believe you can have it. Dream about what you want most, more than anything — qualities, feelings, and experiences in your life and partnership that will bring a smile to your face and warmth to your spirit. Lastly, remember that this is *your* journey, not one taken by you and your current or previous partner. This journey is solo.

Next imagine an anonymous person, a man not yet known in physical form but one you know intimately in your heart. Someone you feel connected to. This is the man who will be your Core Four eventually.

Start the visualization by closing your eyes again, taking a deep breath, and letting your senses lead you to do the following.

See you. . . .
See him. . . .
Smell you. . . .
Smell him. . . .
Hear you. . . .
Hear him. . . .
Feel you. . . .
Feel him. . . .

Allow yourself to really notice you. To notice him. Keep going, and take a journey on which you uncover who this person is — with you, without you, and within the world. Sink into the energy you feel, and imagine the following circumstances.

YOU WITH THIS MAN. What do you look like? How do you feel? Are you peaceful? Passionate? Playful? What is different about you? How does this man's presence enhance your life? Are you expanding or shrinking? How do you behave around him? What is your attitude? Relaxed? Carefree? Serious? Observe how others experience you when you are in this partnership. What do your friends say is the impact of this relationship on you? How well do you maintain your sense of self while you're with him? What is it about being with this man that fills your heart and spirit with joy?

YOU AND HIM TOGETHER, OUT IN THE WORLD. Envision the two of you as a couple in different social situations. How does he interact with others? Notice how he interacts with *you* around others. Observe how others perceive the two of you as a couple. Notice how he touches you, speaks to you, and listens to you in public. What's important to you? What would make you smile from ear to ear? How do you feel being treated this way?

YOU AND HIM TOGETHER, IN PRIVATE SITUATIONS. Hear your conversations. See your daily interactions. Notice the subtle ways he reacts to you. How do you respond to him? How do you feel when you're near him? What's time alone with him like? What's he like when the two of you are connecting, both intimately and otherwise? What is his style of communication? Of connecting to you physically? Emotionally? Mentally? Spiritually? How does he handle difficulty? When does he laugh? When is he tender? How does he support you when life is hard? See him at the very core of his being.

HIM OUT IN THE WORLD WITHOUT YOU, JUST BEING HIMSELF. Notice how he presents himself to the world. Hear what people say about him. Observe how people react to him. Study the types of people he chooses to spend time with. Who are they? Hear what he says about others. Observe how he treats the world and every living thing in it. Feel who he is when he is just being himself.

Discern whether he can be his true self in the world and true to himself in the world.

HIM COMPLETELY ALONE. What does he choose to do with his time alone? Does he know himself? Like himself? What does he love about himself? What does he love to do? What's most important to him? What kind of life does he want to live? How does he define success? Does he want to improve his life? What does this mean to him? Visualize him sitting in total silence, and feel his presence. What does that feel like? Who is he really, inside, and is he willing to show that person to the world?

Now, just stop and let this all sink in, completely imagining and sensing what it is you wish to create. Really embrace the energy you conjured up during the visualization. This is the essence of who this man is with you in your life, and who he is without you, in his soul. Both are important. Make what you saw, smelled, heard, tasted, and felt almost palpable. The energy, and not simply words, will be what makes your Core Four powerful. If you want some extra help with this visualization, you can download an audio recording of it at www.mebeforewe.com. Sometimes it makes a big difference to listen to something instead of reading it.

Step 3. Creating Your Core Four

While you're still holding on to the energy that you just generated through this visualization, it's time to leap into action — a series of five stages that will lead to creating your Core Four. The stages are Reflect; Free Flow; Narrow It Down; Express It; and Try, Revise, Decide. There is no prize for speed. Think of creating your Core Four as an uncovering. The care you take in the process directly determines the end product — just as it does with a well-aged fine wine or a gourmet meal served in several courses, each building on the last. Don't treat your Core Four like a fast-food drive-thru.

Reflect

Before grabbing a pen and paper, think back to all you experienced in your visualization: what you saw, thought, and felt when you imagined this partner.

- What kind of person is he? What does he stand for? What's important to him? What makes him special? How does he treat himself? How does he live? What is at his core?
- How is he in a relationship? How does he relate to you? How does he relate to other people?
- What were you like in the relationship? What did you feel like? How did this particular man enhance your life? Why is he a great partner for *you*?

Free Flow

Now grab that pen and paper. Write down everything you saw, felt, heard, touched, and smelled as you visualized this man. Answer the question "What do I want to manifest in a partner?" Remember, this is the Core Four Free Flow... and this means writing without holding back, letting the floodgates open to anything that comes. Don't stop to judge it. You may find that letting it all come pouring out is a cinch. Or you may need to give yourself a little push to let go, to stop worrying about whether you've given the right answer, or about getting to the Core Four immediately. You'll have time for focusing later, but for now your only objective is to freely express all the qualities, experiences, thoughts, and dreams that surfaced. No editing! Get flowing...

Narrow It Down

Take your Core Four Free-Flow bounty and look through all the words or images recorded on the paper, from beginning to end.

Do it a few times. Start to notice the ones that resonate, and circle those. Begin to see the patterns or similarities among the ones you've circled. Indicate connections by drawing lines between the circled items, or by coloring them with the same color, or by making any other marks that distinguish them. These are your themes.

Get a separate piece of paper and write down all the themes you see, being as verbose as you would like. The goal is not to get to one word but to capture a series of essences, and this requires descriptions, which means multiple words, phrases, and so on. Think of it as painting a picture or telling a story: both evoke emotions and energy in people. Your Core Four will need to do the same.

When you've captured all your themes, assign numbers to them. If you have more than four, that's okay. Setting a goal to get six to eight for the first round is good. If you have fewer than four, you're probably not painting a vivid enough picture. Stop thinking so hard, and let your feelings dictate what you write down! Keep the spirit of the adventurer, and let the energy flow. If you have four, that's great too. Whatever you have, just make sure your themes have enough juice in them to get through the next stage: expression.

Express It

Read through each of your themes, challenging yourself to really feel the energy of the person these words would attract. Your next step is to give each theme a headline that encapsulates the energy and reality you want to evoke. This will be the statement you use in your Core Four. Ask yourself, "What's really important to me about this? What energy do I want to generate? What do these words say about this man's core?" You don't have to get it perfect on the first try; you'll have time to try it on and make alterations. Just do your best to get to the heart of your intention.

Here's an example of one of my Core Four and the themes that produced it. Core Four item: "A man who would sing from the rooftops about how much he loves me." Themes: "A partner who sees all of me and loves me for exactly who I am, all of me. He gives me lots of physical affection and finds me absolutely wonderful — the cat's meow. He's unafraid to show his emotions and his love for me, and for life, in public." Notice that I didn't just pick words like *affectionate* or *a man who appreciates me*. I put soul and color into the words I chose. The description "A man who would sing from the rooftops about how much he loves me" says so many things about the man I have chosen. It says that he is affectionate, appreciative, self-expressive, and grateful, and that he sees me for me. But no one word gets to the spirit of what I actually wanted to manifest. I had to paint a picture and create the energy I was asking to come into my life in the form of a partner. You need to do the same with yours. And by the way, my guy does literally sing, in his deep baritone, show-tune voice — from the sidewalk, the bus, and even out the car window — "I love Christine!"

Let me offer some helpful hints for developing impressions about this partner's essences and putting them into words. Be wary of any surface intentions. Although you may start at a superficial level, don't stop there. Progressively become more intimate with this man and your true desires. For example, one of your four may be: "I want a man who is good with kids." This is a surface intention. Wanting children may indicate some of a man's inner qualities, and may be critical to you, but having kids is ultimately out of your control and not enough to create a fulfilling relationship. Go deeper inside the person you're attracting. Look inside the man you say you want as a life partner. Are you asking for a guy who's loving? Nurturing? A child at heart? Playful? Caring? Whatever qualities you're looking for will exist whether or not you have kids. Get clear about who *he* is. And remember that the Core

Four always work best when they pinpoint the inner qualities of a person, the ones that last a lifetime, not the ones that can be bought or achieved. The latter create a contract; the former, a true partnership.

Also, pay careful attention to verb tense. It matters. I had to reword one of my Core Four from "a person *willing* to grow and experience life fully" to "a person who grows and experiences life fully." Four years into our relationship, I noticed that there were areas of life in which Noah wanted to grow, but in which he was making very little movement. He was always *willing* to grow; he just couldn't act on it. So, I changed the verb tense. Now, I am not suggesting it's the only reason, but believe it or not, he actually shifted and started to grow in those areas. The power of intention at work!

What you should end up with are four (or more, if you are still contemplating) core statements that paint a picture of who this man is. Four (or more) sets of words that evoke emotion in you, and that can be explained with clarity and focus to anyone willing to listen. If you've narrowed your list down to four, check in with your intuition. If she is absolutely sure that these four, just as you've written them, are the best Core Four for you, then move right on to the commitment step. If you're not quite sure that these are the exact four, or if you're still working with more than four, proceed to the next stage and try them on for a while before you decide.

Try, Revise, Decide

This step may take you a few hours or a few weeks. Whatever amount of time it takes, give it to yourself, and promise to finish what you started (that is, choose and commit to your own Core Four). Take the piece of paper with your core statements and put it in a place where you can look at it daily. Ask yourself, "What would my life be like with this guy as my partner, daily and over time? What about these qualities is most important to me? What about these qualities isn't? Don't get crazy analytical about these — that is, stay out of your head and get into your heart. Just look at them each morning, evening, whatever, and ask yourself the three questions.

Revise your core statements as you go, adding and deleting. And when you finally *feel* like you've got them, that your Core Four are true to you, find a new piece of paper and take action: decide. Write your Core Four on this fresh piece of paper, knowing that these are the best expressions of your guy's essence.

Step 4. Making Your Commitment

Nothing will happen unless you tell the universe, "Yes, these are my four! I'm ready to manifest!" Focus and energy won't do you any good without action. It's time to take the next essential step: making a commitment. Committing is your proclamation to the universe: "Yes! This is the partner I want to attract. I am open to receiving this person into my life." It doesn't matter if you currently have a mate; this declaration puts the wheels in motion to create the partnership you *desire*.

The act of committing is an individual choice. Write your final Core Four in a journal or on a sticky note, compose a collage, tell your pet, or send an email blast to all your friends.

Proclaim your choices verbally: "I want to attract a partner who..." Express them silently to yourself over and over again, like a mantra. A friend of mine made an acronym from hers, PILL, and recited it while she did her daily crunches. Whatever floats your boat. Another friend wrote them out and put the piece of paper into a book in her nightstand. At the time, she was single. Six months later, she met her future husband. Later, while she was preparing to move in with her then-fiancé, she found the book with her Core Four in it. It had been two years since her fiancé and she had met, and she'd forgotten about it. Her jaw nearly fell to the floor when she read her Core Four and discovered that her husband-to-be matched every one of them! Today, they are happily married and, more important, they have a wonderful partnership.

Although the action you take is necessary, the specific vehicle is less important than the energy of your commitment. To deliver your intentions to the universe with the power required, you must commit from your heart and spirit, feeling your Core Four in every cell of your body. Your words must ring with vitality, intensity, and passion. Commit with conviction, knowing how truly and honestly you deserve the right guy.

Pick your Core Four and stand by them. Then, as you continue to heal, grow, and learn more about yourself, revisit them. Remember, they aren't written in stone, but you should change them only when you honestly need to. Do it with real thought. Above all, stay grounded in your commitment to yourself. You deserve what you want in partner, so don't settle for less. Do not bend or shift your Core Four so they'll match a certain man. Being single is better than being sorry you hooked up with Mr. Okay.

PART *Three*

WE ♥

CHAPTER Seven

Getting Wise about WE

FOUR SHORTCUTS TO CREATING AUTHENTIC PARTNERSHIPS INSTEAD OF UNHEALTHY RELATIONSHIPS

*W*elcome to the final part of our adventure. For the next two chapters, our attention will focus on WE. Notice that our purpose has been to choose ME *before* WE, not *instead of* WE. This is because relationships can be a fantastic part of our lives, as long as we remember that a relationship is not a requirement, it's a choice. I believe that an informed choice is always the best kind — whether the information comes from our intuition, the sage wisdom of another, or our own experiences. The last several chapters have informed you about ME and HE. As your guide on this journey, I would be remiss if I didn't give you the chance to learn more about WE. Sometimes people don't know what they're missing, or even what's possible, until someone points the way. I always knew I wanted more from my relationships, and there was a time when I didn't know exactly what that "more" was. When you can't articulate what you want, it's a heck of a lot harder to create it.

Let's explore some of what's possible in a relationship, beyond what you might have created in the past. Two things I think most women want in relationships are partnership and intimacy, but few of us ever actually get them. Those of us who do end up with fulfilling relationships based on authentic partnership and mutual intimacy arrive there only after a lot of trial and error (and usually bumps and bruises). I hope to provide you with thoughts, inquiries, and stories that will inform your relationship choices for the rest of your life. I've written these in the form of four "shortcuts." They're shortcuts because, if you take them, you'll avoid a lot of unnecessary suffering and wasted time. You'll also increase the likelihood of creating what you really want, instead of having to simply react to what you find yourself living in. And, of course, they all start with ME.

The following discussion is about being in a relationship, but all points are applicable to whatever your mate status is. The information I offer will help you determine what you want and where you are, at all points in your life. So if you're single, you can check in with yourself and see what you believe to be true today, or you can use a previous relationship, or more than one, in your reflections. If you're in a relationship, use your current and/or past relationships to see the truth today as well as the patterns you've been following. Whatever your status, always keep this question in mind as you study the shortcuts: "How have the ideas discussed in this shortcut influenced my current or past relationships?" Compare the recommendations in the shortcut with your beliefs and ideals and ask yourself, "What is true for ME?"

Shortcut 1: Avoid Unhealthy Attraction and Choose Authentic Partnership

We have all witnessed the woman who meets a man, falls instantly in love, gets swept away, and starts professing things like "forever," "*the* one," and "living together," only to end up heartbroken months later. It comes as no surprise to us. We knew all along that failure was inevitable, or at least probable. Being a good friend, we tried to save her, to warn her. We may have tried to tell her that the two of them hadn't had enough time to really get to know each other, let alone profess their status as soul mates. Yes, they were crazy about each other, and the chemistry was real, but we knew (or judged) that this relationship, fueled by unsustainable, perhaps unhealthy, attraction was doomed. Sadly, it's hard to wake a starry-eyed friend up before her heart gets broken, but our lack of success may not be due to a lack of effort. When a woman has been swept off her feet, the last thing she wants is someone trying to get her feet out of the glass slippers of her fantasy and into the shoes of her reality.

We tell ourselves that if it were us in the same situation, we'd never turn a deaf ear to the wise words of friends. But let's face it, we have *all* had our own unhealthy attractions and superficial connections, even if our own stories were not of the exciting whirlwind-romance variety. And I suppose, if all we wanted from our relationships was sex, dinner, and stimulating conversation, we could keep our delusions about these unhealthy attractions alive for years, without any serious ramifications. But while great sex, food, and conversation can be very satisfying, this is not what most women are looking for.

Whether we know it or not, when it comes to relationships, the majority of us desire, even yearn for, *authentic partnerships*. And while it's easier to experience such a partnership than to define it, I can offer you a simple definition from the dictionary of my life:

Authentic partnership (*aw-then-tik parht-ner-ship*) n. A dynamic, life-*affirming* connection based on intimacy, respect, trust, truth, unconditional love, and friendship.

It's authentic because the relationship and the two people in it are real — about themselves and the relationship. It's a partnership because there is mutuality — both people lean into the relationship and each other, over and over again, hand in hand. It's life-affirming because it makes each person's life better, giving energy to both rather than sucking it out of them. It's dynamic because it's always growing and evolving, as are the two people in it.

In my estimation, if we're interested in joining with a HE to form a WE, whether this means a boyfriend, husband, or companion, there is no good reason to accept anything other than authentic partnership. We don't *need* a partner, but if we're going to have one, why choose anything but an authentic one? Women can and do build fantastic and fulfilling lives alone. As single women, we can get along just fine, counting on our friends and family for support and nourishment, and on ourselves to create the lives we dream about. We *choose* to be in relationship with a man for a reason. We desire an intimate bond, a companion, a person to laugh and cry and grow with, a true partner committed to being in life *with* us, someone to see the deepest parts of our soul, whose presence encourages us to be our best ME. It may be human nature to crave connection, but if we're looking for more than steamy sex or a book club partner, we owe it to ourselves to accept nothing less than an authentic partnership, and this requires *healthy* attraction.

Attraction — physical, emotional, intellectual, spiritual — is important, really important. None of us wants to hang out with a guy who makes our stars fizzle or our minds yawn, but attraction must be healthy to create a great, or even a good, relationship. And the only way to determine if your attraction is of the healthy variety is to get downright honest about what inspired the connection. Of course no woman wants to jump up and down exclaiming, "Look at me over here! I am dying to expose my messed up relationship!" but if we don't get real about the health of our attractions, we risk losing what's more important than anything else — our selves.

One reason we often mistake unhealthy attraction for the healthy connections found in authentic partnerships is that most of us have never thought about it. When was the last time you sat down for a cup of tea and said, "I think I'll define what 'authentic partnership' means to me today"? Even among those who have considered the source of their connection, most haven't been truthful about how healthy their attraction is or isn't. So, ignorant, blind, or in denial, we end up living in the grips of unhealthy attraction, feeling like something is missing or wrong, lacking the words to articulate what that something is. If we're lucky, after lots of pain and suffering caused by the times we engaged in unhealthy attraction, we finally free ourselves and learn about our desire for a partnership.

I have met more smart and successful women than I care to admit who've lost their minds, and themselves, in the throes of unhealthy attraction. I've watched many a wise woman lodge a guy so deep in her wounds that she mistakes the resulting feelings for the authentic partnership she was waiting for. Maybe for some the unhealthy attraction feels so fabulous because their catch comes with a first-class ticket to social status and financial security, filling their holes that come from the absence of self-worth or the fear of lack. Or maybe the man they meet seemingly gives them permission to be the wild child they always wanted to be but their parents never allowed, filling in their holes caused by never feeling like they fit with their family. Regardless of our individual stories and corresponding wounds, when in the clutches of an unhealthy attraction, we are too entangled in our feelings to see the truth. We need to know the warning signs beforehand. Commit the following signals to memory and keep them for future reference.

Warning Signs of Unhealthy Attraction

HOLE-STUFFING JUNKIE. Without a doubt, it's our emotions, hormones, and emotional wounds that control the show here. The feelings swirling inside our bodies and psyches are so intense that it seems impossible to control our actions or stop making self-destructive decisions. Convinced that this guy is the love of our life, we experience the relationship as if it were a drug, and we become like a junkie. The man becomes the fix for our external needs and gaping holes, and the bigger our emotional holes, the more intensely we feel drawn to and attached to this man. The physical connection is usually undeniable, like a gravitational pull we can't control. And our emotional and intellectual fantasies run rampant, which is why most women mistake these unhealthy relationships for authentic partnerships. But unlike healthy connections, which support us and encourage us to be our full and authentic selves, the unhealthy bonds lead to devastating and life-draining lows. While the ride may feel good at times, in the end we are too often left unsatisfied, sad, and empty, with our desires and needs unmet. The cycle is always the same: we give in to the intense attraction, fall totally into it and enjoy the highs, plummet to the depths of despair, and then start the cycle all over again. While it may feel fantastic at times to be intertwined with the other, using him to avoid healing our wounds is unhealthy.

COTTON BALLS IN MY EARS. This guy is "the one," and we will vehemently profess to those closest to us that "HE is the love of my life, I don't care what you say!... If *you* really loved me, you would be happy for me.... You just don't understand." Convinced that we know the real deal even if our friends and family think otherwise, we won't listen to what anyone has to say. Sure, the relationship isn't perfect — he's got a girlfriend, he lies, he has an addiction problem, or he's not committing anytime soon — but because we have great chemistry or some other "special" connection, we're convinced that the rest of the world just doesn't know what they're talking about. What most of us need when we're in this state is a bucket of cold water in the face to wake us the hell up! If our friends and family scream, "Stop!" and we don't listen, it's almost a sure bet that our relationship is not a healthy influence.

THE DERANGED LOVE TRAIN. Our heads fill with thoughts like "Who cares that we just met three weeks ago? He told me that he loves me, and I love him." We believe without a glimmer of doubt that we are in LOVE. Sure, the feelings are undeniably powerful, and the sex fantastic, so how could it be anything but love? Warning! When we start asking ourselves questions like "How would his last name sound with mine?" "What will our babies be named?" and "Where will we live?" weeks into our relationship, we have just entered fantasyland. Even if this man is playing along, and even if you really are meant to be life partners, questions like this do not belong anywhere near the beginning of a relationship. There is no getting around the fact that we cannot be in love with someone we don't really know. Intensely attracted, you bet, but in love, no. Love and authentic partnership take time.

Antidotes for Unhealthy Attraction

While unhealthy attraction may feel great, liberating, and even life-giving at times, in the end the great feelings are not sustainable. They may, however, keep us in a relationship for years, preventing us from finding the kind of relationship we really desire. Luckily for us, there are extremely powerful antidotes to the unhealthy attraction syndrome, which all entail being truthful to ourselves — and admittedly, this is usually easier said than done.

One of the most effective ways to snap ourselves out of the

unhealthy delusions of our attraction is to stop and question ourselves. Automatically, whether we're in a relationship or single, it
forces us to turn our focus away from HE and WE, and place it
directly on ME. And as we've learned, the only way we can create what we want is to be real with ourselves, even when it isn't
easy. So if you find yourself in a WE, even if things are going great,
stop and answer the following questions from time to time. Challenge yourself to be 100 percent honest, even if — especially if —
you don't like the answers.

ANTIDOTE 1:

Why do you want a HE and a WE in your life?

ANTIDOTE 2:

What kind of HE and WE do you currently have?
Does what you have fit what you want?

ANTIDOTE 3:

If it fits, great. If what you have doesn't fit, what line of
bull are you feeding yourself to make it okay to stay?
In what ways are you settling?

Every woman deserves a dynamic, life-affirming partnership,
but many of us settle for less, and as a result, we get a relationship,
not a partnership. We stay with men we connect with or are
attracted to, but who are not walking with us down life's path as
authentic partners — we aren't supporting each other, enriching
each other's experiences, and nourishing each other's spirit and
heart. When the relationship moves past the dating stage and into
the more serious living-life-together phase, unless it's a partnership, most women will find themselves dealing with life's demands
alone. Because we can, we forge ahead, attempting to carry the
burden of the entire load, putting our own needs last and ending
up tired as hell. My experience of doing it alone while in a relationship was that it had far too great a cost to my soul. No matter

how attracted we are to a guy, if he's a dead weight, an emotionally empty vessel, or toxic sewage in our energy streams, then he
has no place in our lives.

I gained a deeper understanding of the choice to settle for an
unhealthy attraction as I watched my dear friend Jill repeat her version of my own past relationship. She lived unhappily with a man
she was attracted to, who was never a partner to her creative, lively,
and beautiful spirit.

Jill's Story

A terrific writer with a hilarious sense of humor and stunning
red hair, Jill grew up in a world of debutant balls. But if you
met her, you would never sense her privileged background.
With her engaging personality, Jill is the kind of girl anyone
could talk with for hours over coffee. She dated an interesting array of men until, when she was thirty, Mike appeared.
He aggressively pursued her. They dated for several months,
he moved in, then they married, bought a new house, and had
two children.

A few years into their marriage, when she couldn't live
in the "happy illusion" any longer, Jill told me that, on the
night she first met Mike, a voice inside her had practically
shouted, "Do not go out with this guy. He is trouble. He will
mess up your life!" She recalled the clarity of this warning and
described how she had felt it in her bones. But, as so many of
us do, Jill chose to ignore the voice and let her attraction to
Mike overpower her intuition. At the time, she saw this guy
as a unique combination of intense businessman and social
rebel. He was a financially successful lawyer who had the
potential for acquiring money and power, aspects of life she

had grown up with. But what interested her most was the combination of his aptitude for success with a scrappy, nonconformist personality. Mike was not the typical yuppie or a slick corporate guy; he was irreverent, and, like her, he didn't fit the mold. Jill was charmed by his intelligence and creativity, which complemented her wit and aspirations to become a novelist.

Today, Jill admits that Mike satisfied her need for financial prosperity and good social status, as well as her desire to live differently from the upper-class world in which she grew up. She wanted to live an interesting life in a city full of eclectic people, not be a country club wife, but she also wanted to be as successful as the people from her background. It all sounds good, so far. However, fitting into both worlds was unhealthily important to Jill — and her need to do so related mostly to the childhood holes she had yet to heal. Jill used Mike's successful rebellion to fill her holes, and this allowed her to exist in both worlds without having to deal with her wounds.

At the time she married Mike, Jill knew nothing about hole stuffing. Nor did she understand what she *really* desired in a man. Unhealthy and unaware, she couldn't see that Mike was not the man her spirit craved, that what she actually wanted was a person who saw her soul, nurtured and adored her, and supported her creative desires, one who showed up to build a life with her *together* — a partner.

A few years into their marriage, after a series of miscarriages and the death of three grandparents, Jill turned off the autopilot and began to become self-aware. The material success she had believed would make her happy disappeared when Mike lost his job and struggled in his career. She had to become the main breadwinner to keep the family afloat, *and* she gave birth to the kids, took care of them, kept the house organized, grieved her losses, and tried to manage her life. Her dream of writing short stories and novels began to disappear, as did any sign of Mike stepping up to be her partner. When she could no long hide her loneliness, despair, and exhaustion, she was forced to see that, although she loved Mike, something was missing.

Jill's life force was being sucked dry. Her hair actually turned from a lustrous red to the color and texture of straw. Tired, frazzled, and running a nonstop marathon, she found that, no matter how much she did, her life remained a chaotic mess. That's when she had to face the truth — she had chosen a husband, but not a partner. She had settled for too little. Mike did not support her needs — he took more than he gave. Sure, he understood her intellectual and emotional triggers intimately, but he never saw her soul. He was never the man with whom she could create the life she wanted.

Jill tried to make the relationship work, but Mike was willing to make only small changes and would not participate in the deep personal work required. She continued working on herself, healing and becoming more self-aware. After many failed attempts to change Mike and the marriage, she filed for divorce. It was not an easy decision, especially with two young daughters, but she felt that being a woman who loved herself was one of the most important examples she could set for her children.

What surprised Jill most after making the decision to divorce Mike was that her attraction to him remained.

Emotionally and intellectually, she still gravitated to him from time to time, even though she knew their relationship brought her misery and loneliness. In due time, Jill came to understand that she didn't really miss Mike; her feelings came from the open wounds that he no longer filled for her. As she continued to heal, her attraction to Mike faded. It didn't disappear overnight, but as she took responsibility for her own life, the reality of who Mike had always been overpowered any illusions of a romantic bond.

We owe it to ourselves to ask questions like: "Do my partner and I have a deeply *intimate*, not just *intense*, relationship?" "What is the source of our attraction? Is our relationship based on unhealthy or healthy attraction — physically, emotionally, intellectually, and spiritually?" and "Is this relationship really a partnership? Is it based on trust, respect, trust, friendship, and mutuality?" And we should be able to answer these questions honestly.

♥ ME Reflections ♥

At some point, each of us must find the truth in our own lives and look at our relationships with complete honesty, just as Jill did. What is your story?

- What do you really want? Unhealthy attraction or an authentic partnership with healthy attraction? Or something else?

- Think back through all your relationships. When have you mistaken unhealthy attraction for authentic partnership? What was the effect on you and your life? What was it about you that allowed you to fall into the attraction trap?

- What do you believe is the essential foundation for a healthy, dynamic, and authentic partnership? How does that differ from what you have now or from your last serious relationship?

- Think about your current relationship or one you had in the past. What do you or did you have? What is or was the source of your connection? What are the healthy or unhealthy attractions — physically, emotionally, intellectually, and spiritually?

- Which of the following authentic-partnership pieces are present in your relationship, and which ones are missing? Respect? Truth? Intimacy? Mutuality (active and equal participation by both partners)? Think about what these words really mean at their core. Challenge yourself to hold your relationship to the highest standard.

If you desire authentic partnership, you owe it to yourself to ask for it and not settle for less. If you proclaim that you aren't looking for intimacy or partnership, finding a guy who'll be just a sex toy or intellectual debater might be exactly right. But then be honest about your expectations — good times with a guy you're intensely attracted to are great, if that's what you want. Hell, sometimes we aren't ready for or don't want a partnership. But in that case, don't complain that the deep connection of partnership is missing. Know what you want. Be honest about what you have. And if you don't like your situation, take responsibility for it and do something to change it.

Shortcut 2: Authentic Partnerships Take More Than Love

Love alone, like attraction alone, is not enough to create a fulfilling, dynamic, life-affirming partnership. Love is a prerequisite, of course, but it's not *the* reason to choose a man as a mate. Yet when we're asked why we want to marry, be with, have children with, and sleep with the guy we're involved with, our first response is often "Because I love him." While it sounds like the right answer, make no mistake, it's a danger signal worthy of attention. Red alert!

Think about all the men you've loved, relatives and friends excluded. Remember, with honesty, why you never walked down the aisle with any of them. Or if you did, consider why the relationship didn't work. Chances are, the union ended not because you didn't love the man but because of personal differences, illusions, hole stuffing, dishonesty, unhealthy patterns, or a lack of self-awareness, intimacy, trust, or respect. If love were all a person needed to have a great marriage, there'd be far fewer divorces.

What is your emotional reaction to the idea that love isn't enough of a reason to make a commitment to a man and a relationship? Are you open to the idea, or does skepticism, indifference, or irritation blur your vision? This shortcut makes a lot of people uncomfortable, defensive, and sometimes even argumentative, and it's meant to. The notion that love is not enough is what I call a poker, an idea or question that challenges you to be real about any illusions you have on the topic, ultimately freeing you to experience new possibilities. This poker gives you the opportunity to look more deeply at your motivations for picking a specific man, beyond love. So if you're feeling poked — good! Gaining this clarity is worth any discomfort the inquiry brings. The power of a poker lies in the fact that it makes you stop and think, "What is true for me?" If it's a good poker, the inquiry will help you recognize the unhealthy beliefs, actions, and lies, so that you can actually discard them and create what you really want. If you're not totally sold on this idea that love isn't enough to create an authentic partnership, no worries. All I ask is that you play along and look at what I've found to be true for me and many, many other women — and allow yourself to discover what is true for you.

So why does authentic partnership require more than love? People love according to their capacity to give and receive love. This capacity is directly linked to how much a person will or won't allow respect, truth, intimacy, and trust into his or her life. The real difference between a relationship based on the *ideal* of love, and an authentic partnership in which love is part of the foundation, is the answer to the question "Why *this* guy?" When your answer includes such things as respect, trust, support, friendship, and connection, the warning bells are silent. Not because there's more love in this relationship, but because you both have the ability to share your selves, your feelings, and your lives. Quite frankly, when we have the ability to trust, be respectful (in the most difficult situations), and be vulnerably honest, we can love *better*, which has nothing to do with loving someone more.

Respect, truth, intimacy, and trust are big ideas, and I could probably write an entire tome on each one. Thankfully for us, we're all about shortcuts in this chapter, so I've included the Cliffs Notes version for respect and truth, to help you broaden your understanding of what, beyond love, is required for a great WE. We'll talk more about intimacy and trust in the next chapter.

Respect

You show respect when, in *all* interactions, you remain open to what the other person has to say, even when — especially when — you disagree. No matter how much you want to squirm away, blast your partner to pieces, or cut his position to shreds, you listen to his words with an open mind and heart. You let the words penetrate your defensive barriers and, ultimately, impact your response. "Why in the world would I want to do that?" you may ask. Because, believe it or not, even in the heat of an argument our partner's words may change how we feel or think and therefore what we decide to say. Too often as we listen to our guy, we are formulating our attack or holding back just long enough to store up momentum to pounce. We employ phrases like missiles, spouting statements such as "Last year, you did...," or "I am always the one who... and you never...," and of course, "You've done it to me before, remember..." (Reference to the past as a way to rub a person's face into it is never respectful and is not part of an authentic partnership.) Without deep respect for our beloved, our interactions are like highly charged fencing matches without rules for fighting fair. With respect, any interaction, even the most difficult one, can be more like a dynamic dance in which each is a leader and a follower — it's a partnership in which we travel through life together, each respecting the movement of the other.

Truth

Truth is present in a relationship when you can really tell the other person what you're honestly feeling or thinking. No matter how vulnerable, ashamed, or scared you feel, you say what's on your mind and in your heart, with respect of course. Many times, in the name of truth, we lacerate our partners or bang them over the head with our points of view — that's not the kind of truth I'm talking about. Truth is honest and can be very blunt, but it's never malicious, although sometimes it hurts. Truth can't happen if your pattern is to suppress your emotions, letting them bubble under the surface until they explode like a volcano. Authentic partnerships demand that we wear our emotions and thoughts on our sleeves, expressing them in the moment, from our hearts rather than from our defensive egos. If we can't be 100 percent unconditionally honest with our partners, we don't really have partners, and we probably don't have a healthy relationship with ourselves.

In the relationship I had with my ex-person, as I became more self-aware I began to see that our love didn't create respect, honesty, or intimacy, which of course contributed to my tremendous loneliness. Yet I still loved him. This love is what kept me trying to make our relationship work, thinking that if we just believed in our love for each other, the rest would fall into place. It never did. The irony, of course, is that, although our union ended in a shambles, the fact that I loved him didn't change.

❤ ME Reflections ❤

* What are your ideals about love?
* When have you used these ideals, in the absence of respect, truth, or trust, as the reason to build a deeper commitment with your guy? What was the result?
* What do respect, truth, and trust mean to you? Why are they important to you? When have you settled for less, and why?

Shortcut 3: Love Alone Is Never a Reason to Stay

If love alone is not enough to make a long-lasting, fulfilling partnership, it is certainly not a good enough reason to stay in a relationship. However, for many of us, love is exactly why we stay longer than we should in relationships that don't meet our needs or desires. Our reasoning? "If I love this man and he loves me in return, that's enough, no matter how exhausted, unhappy, or lonely I feel." Even if we know that our guy will never be a true partner, we hang around because "I love him." We forfeit our joy and life dreams all because we're in love. But love should never require sacrificing one's self. Surrendering one's self is the antithesis of choosing ME before WE.

So why do we choose to stay in unfulfilling relationships that push ME aside? Having stayed a mind-boggling fourteen years too long in one myself, I think the biggest reason is fear. We are desperately afraid that, if we leave a man who says he loves us, we will never find someone to love us again. Sacrificing joy and happiness becomes a small price to pay to avoid the thought of living "alone." The more thoroughly this guy is stuffed into our holes, the greater the terror of ending the connection. We hang on, hoping that our mate will change and become the true partner we want. As long as there is a glimmer of possibility, we attempt to survive in any relationship.

Our most useful coping strategy becomes finding excuses to stay. Like a magician, we pull reasons out of the hat to justify continuing the relationship. Month after month, year after year, we create new arguments for staying. And while many of our illusions disappear over time, one rationalization always remains — love. We stay because we love him. For most of us, love becomes enough, because it must. Without love, the only option is to leave. And unless we've conquered our fear of being alone or have learned to love ourselves enough to choose ME before WE, breaking off the relationship seems almost worse than dying. We convince ourselves that "of course we should stay together; we love each other. That's what's most important." Regardless of how destructive or unsatisfying the relationship, if the love stays, we stay.

If we wait for the love to disappear before deciding a relationship has run its course, we will cling forever. Love doesn't go away. Sure, sometimes the force of anger, regret, betrayal, and hate catapults us out of a relationship, but love remains under all the hurtful emotions. We can vehemently dislike how a man has treated us or who he has become, and still love him. We can be so angry with our former mate for not living up to his end of our agreement, and still love him. One of the biggest fallacies in our society is that people fall out of love. Love *changes* and *shifts*, sure, but people *fall out* of respect, intimacy, and trust. They don't fall out of love.

I still love the man who broke my heart. Even after the awful experience of our breakup, I still love him. I don't respect the actions he took as our relationship ended, and I would never trust him again, but I don't need to. All my illusions and codependent patterns are gone. I don't think about him every day or long for him. I am done with our relationship forever, because I have healed ME. My choice to be okay with our relationship ending has nothing to do with love; if it did, I would have run into his arms when he called a year after our breakup asking me to get back together with him. I said no, not because I didn't love him, but because I knew the relationship was never going to be right for me. Several times during our fifteen-year dance, I went back for love, but I would never make that mistake again. I had all the love I needed, from ME; what I wanted in a man was a partner, and he wasn't it.

We can love a man and choose not to be with him. Making this decision can actually be our healthiest option, especially when our mate is headed in a different direction, is blind to our magnificence, or isn't the partner we truly desire. If leaving frees us to create the life we want, then it is our best choice, much better than waiting around for a man to be someone he's not, while we silently yearn — or perhaps badger him in passive-aggressive ways — for more than love alone can provide.

When a relationship ends, we may not feel love at the time, but it will keep breathing underneath the intense hurt and feelings of rejection. Once we process our pain and fear, love becomes the emotion that heals us. The wounds don't close overnight, but with time, when we can again find love in our hearts, nothing more powerfully transforms hurt into freedom from the past than love does.

As my friend Jill went through the dissolution of her marriage, she and I came to understand how so many of us stay far too long, grasping for new reasons to keep the relationship afloat. Jokingly, we started to refer to this self-created phenomenon as "love poker," a game where we are both dealer and player, flipping cards and raising the ante to keep the game, our relationship, alive.

Although Jill stayed married to Mike for five years, thoughts of leaving him had surfaced within the first two years of their marriage. Throughout her marriage, Jill engaged in a mad game of love poker. In her mind, she dealt a deck of cards, back and forth, trying to find the right hand to make the marriage work — drawing new cards, folding, trying over, and raising the stakes. Jill would throw in the "I love him" chip, telling herself, "I love him, so maybe I *shouldn't* leave." Then she would raise the stakes: "I love him, so why *would* I leave? Maybe I'm being crazy and unreasonable." Next came the card "Maybe he really will change. I see progress, perhaps he will make the big shifts I've been waiting for."

No matter how many hands Jill played, or how often the game seemed to turn in her favor, Mike never came through. Jill's needs were left unmet, and she and Mike would squabble, fight, and arm-wrestle for control.

The game didn't stop, not even after she made the decision to end the marriage. Sure, there were many days when Jill had the strength to see clearly, and she would remember why she was divorcing Mike. But then he would do something thoughtful, or she would get scared, and she would end up back at the love poker table, where she always lost.

Jill kept the game going until one day — almost a year and a half after she had declared her desire for a divorce — she finally began to understand that love had nothing to do with her reasons for leaving Mike. She finally got that she was always going to love him, and that she still loved many of the qualities that originally had attracted her to him. Much to her surprise, these physical, intellectual, and emotional connections didn't disappear overnight. And finally, Jill came to understand that she would always love Mike, *and* that she didn't want to be married to him any longer. Both were true. Interestingly, with that insight, the love became healthier. It was no longer based on an attachment to Mike changing or the relationship working. Her love for Mike now stemmed from the good memories, their children, and what she learned about herself from their relationship. As she healed her holes, the emotional and intellectual attraction faded, but the love remained.

Shortcut 4: Ending a Relationship Is Not Failure; Failure Is Trying to Keep a Dead One Alive

Another friend of mine shared a wise thought after my relationship with my ex-person ended. I had believed with all my heart that my guy and I were *supposed* to be together forever. And I felt that, because our partnership had not lasted, it was a total failure and fifteen years of my life had been wasted. Wrong. My sage friend's wisdom was this: Life is like a sidewalk. We walk down the sidewalk of our lives, sometimes alone, sometimes with others. With certain people we travel many miles, until they turn down a different street, marching on without us into their own futures. Other friends, lovers, and acquaintances, we stroll with for a short while, and then they detour on their paths. And still others we walk with for a very long time, maybe to the end of our street, the end of our lives. No matter who we walk with or the length of the journey together, the path we travel is always our own.

These words influenced my perception of relationships profoundly. I came to understand that every situation lasts for as long as it's meant to be. Endings are a natural part of life. Things start and end, over and over again. Because each of us has an individual path, our own life, we continuously walk with different people through the stages of our lives. Some travel with us forever, and others are called to different paths. When the person we walk with chooses to take an alternate route, the decision is not personal; we all must be true to our own paths.

Unfortunately, this thinking escapes most of our society. We are raised to believe in "forever" relationships, conditioned to stay with a man even when we're unhappy. We are sold a bill of goods that says, if a relationship doesn't last for the rest of your life, it's a failure, and failing in our society is unacceptable. This whacked-out rationalization keeps us in relationships long past the time they should end, just so we can avoid the feeling and judgment of failure. The only honorable choice seems to be to "fight to the death" to make the partnership work.

But there is another option: we can believe that people come into our lives for many reasons, and that *every* relationship is a teacher. The lessons may be short and painful; medium and sweet; long and empowering; or never-ending and continuously torturous. Regardless of *how* a relationship teaches us, its success doesn't depend on the relationship lasting forever. It's a success when we become *aware* of the reason for having this man in our life. Great fortune is available to us when we understand that our relationship serves us in some way, good or bad. When we can step back and see the dynamic of our partnership as a wise teacher, we can learn from it and make a self-aware choice either to keep it or to eliminate it from our life. If we choose to end a bond with someone, we may be sad, but terminating the relationship does not denote failure. Rather, we can be grateful for the lessons it taught us, for making us smarter, healthier, and more self-aware. We can choose gratitude over embarrassment or shame.

A few years ago, a friend of mine moved in with her boyfriend of one year. Their relationship rocked! Authentic partnership all the way. But it almost came to a screeching halt during their first month of cohabitation, when they found themselves completely attached to the idea of their relationship "working," to it "lasting." At first they didn't realize that both of them had huge expectations, and they acted out their discomfort in juvenile, and frankly common, ways. She freaked out about "his" stuff being in "her" apartment. And they both freaked out about their different ways of handling money: she had five years of historical financial data on her computer, and he didn't even have a computer, let alone balance his checkbook. Separately, they each silently wondered if they had made a very bad decision to cohabitate.

After a month of their escalating freak-out, their ability to communicate and their willingness to be honest and vulnerable trumped their panic and fear, and they had "the conversation." It was a moment of trust when they both shared their feelings and concerns, and it ultimately allowed them to see the tremendous pressure they had been putting on themselves to make this relationship work. Both had been fully attached to the idea of being the other's "one," and both deeply desired to keep this love in their lives — but it was this attachment that was strangling their partnership. They realized something had to change.

So they made a commitment to stay together for as long as it was good for both of them. If at any time one was unhappy, that person would come forth before deciding to just end the partnership. They also agreed that, even if their relationship didn't work out, they would both be okay. Sad, but okay. This realization and commitment lifted a ton of pressure off each person as well as the relationship.

We all have the ability to free ourselves of the heavy burden of "forever" and to look at our relationship through a new lens. We can choose to commit to our relationship for as long as it is right and good for us. We can vow that, if for some reason the WE changes, we will be honest with ME and our partner. As long as we are truthful and open with each other and ourselves, our relationship can never be a failure.

❤ ME Reflections ❤

- What do you believe about relationships lasting forever? About what makes a relationship a failure?
- Are you attached to the idea of your current relationship lasting forever? When have you been attached to "forever" in previous relationships? What was the impact on you and your life?
- What beliefs about the notion of "forever" would you like to change? About what failure in a relationship is or isn't? Are you willing to release your attachment to "forever" in all relationships?
- What gifts have you received from relationships that are no longer part of your life? How can you apply them to current or future relationships?

Remember, long-lasting partnerships that fulfill our hearts and spirits enhance our lives. If we're awake, then satisfying and enduring partnerships are possible. Our *attachment* to the idea of our unions lasting forever is what summons undue pressure and keeps us in situations long past the time they should have ended.

Delving Deeper
WHAT DO YOU WANT IN A WE?

With these new shortcuts in your WE toolbox, you're better prepared to create the kind of relationship you want. So of course the next logical step is to get really clear on what you want in a relationship. We've talked about some of the components of authentic partnerships, but what is true for you?

My challenge to you is to sink into this question: What do you really want in your relationship? Let yourself feel, and then express, what comes. And express it with passion and emotion, with your heart and soul. Complete the following statement:

My WE is…

Maybe you'll produce a verbal answer, or maybe a journal entry. Or perhaps you'll create a painting, a collage, or even a song, remembering that what you focus on and put energy into, you create.

CHAPTER  Eight

Getting the Intimacy We Crave

IF WE WANT IT, WE MUST BE WILLING TO GIVE IT FIRST

We play a critical part in creating intimacy in our partnerships. We must be willing and able to both give *and* ask for intimate connection, and this requires us to be honest and vulnerable. How can we expect to receive that which we cannot give? We can't. It's time to take responsibility for our part in creating the WE our hearts and spirits desire, because the truth is, intimacy starts with ME.

Unfortunately, although we desperately crave connection and intimacy, most of us are too damn afraid to speak freely enough from our hearts to get it. Instead, we talk from our heads and our fears, unwilling to open the door to our innermost feelings, which keeps us from saying the things we really need and want to say. We are like kindergartners when it comes to the skills necessary to be vulnerable with our partners, to openly communicate, or to own our real feelings. The result? We actually prevent the intimacy we hunger for most, and we settle for much less.

Our biggest obstacle to intimacy is ME — our own fear of rejection, abandonment, and criticism. When fear rules our emotions and thoughts, intimacy is impossible and vulnerability cannot exist. Luckily, there is another alternative: *choose* to be truthful and vulnerable, and *insist* that your partner be the same.

Building an intimate partnership isn't always easy — it takes self-awareness, time, and trust. But it's totally possible. In fact, learning to create intimacy is one of the greatest benefits of being in a partnership. Intimacy with another person opens us up so we can live more and love more of ourselves. I'd even go so far as to say that intimate relationships are so magical and fulfilling that no woman should go a lifetime without one. I've lived both ways: deeply craving intimacy and fully basking in it. While the latter takes more vulnerability, it's infinitely worth the price. Vulnerability doesn't come easy for most, and it certainly didn't for me. I've been working on letting my walls down since the day I realized that the intimacy I was pushing away was exactly what I'd been craving. One of the first things I learned was that, while I'd pushed intimacy away many times, I'd never pushed it away more aggressively than when, as my therapist pointed out to me, "my fear of abandonment" went into overdrive.

This deep-seated fear limited the depth of my connection with my guy, Noah, for the first few years of our relationship. When it wasn't in the foreground causing a ruckus, it was waiting in the background for a moment when it could. One of its favorite times to show up was whenever Noah was getting ready to leave on a trip without me (in other words, to "abandon me"). It wasn't that I consciously thought he would never come back; I just couldn't help picking a fight big enough to create an emotional chasm between us before he left.

As if that wasn't enough, I'd repeat the pattern all over again on his return. Always, moments before he was due home, my heart would start palpitating with joy, but on seeing him, I'd find that my emotional chasm had reappeared. More than anything, I wanted to hug him exuberantly, to shower him with affection, and to exclaim, "I missed you so much!" but the words wouldn't come. Instead, I'd give him a nice hug and a friendly "Welcome home." It would take hours for me to break down the wall around my heart enough to let him inside and to create the space for us to reconnect.

Once I became aware of this destructive pattern, I really tried to change my behavior but made only slight progress at best. Luckily, the universe has a way of lending a hand when we are struggling. However, it can often feel more like a shove. My not-so-gentle push came on the day Noah left for a nine-day retreat, the first in which we would have absolutely no communication. While he was away, my abandonment monster lost its mind! And true to form, within fifteen minutes of Noah's return, I swung into full fear mode. When Noah walked in the door smiling ear to ear, happy beyond words to see me, I could have invited him to share his enlightening, life-changing experiences with me, but instead, my defense system went wild. All I saw was a man filled with hope and new ideas who was clearly going to leave me to pursue some sort of personal life mission. So I did what any girl in the grips of fear would do: I decided to push him away first.

For me that meant putting my defense mechanism of choice — control — in gear and spewing demands and ultimatums like "If you think I am leaving San Francisco, you're crazy!" and "You can leave, but I am staying right here!" (Noah had never uttered a word about changing his job or moving to a new city.) When I stopped my tirade long enough to see Noah's face, I was struck by the utter bewilderment of his expression. In that moment, I realized how out of control I was. All Noah really wanted was to share his life and new experiences with the woman he loved — me — and all I could do was think of myself and push him away. Not a

CHOOSING ME before WE

successful formula for intimate connection! A better choice would have been for me to express my fears, to show my vulnerability.

Fortunately, the intensity of this experience woke me up to how much damage my fear of abandonment was causing. I had always consciously understood that Noah wasn't leaving me, but my subconscious had taken control. I knew that to change this dynamic, I had to start with ME, and that I also needed the support of WE. So, WE practiced, before and after every trip, speaking honestly about my emotions and fears. Separately, I focused on healing the holes caused by my fear of abandonment.

Eventually, I was able to make a permanent and significant shift, in large part because Noah offered a safe space for me to be vulnerable, without judgment or blame. And that's what intimacy requires — for each person in the relationship to invite the other partner in and not slam the door when the gremlins get riled. How often do we start to connect with loving intentions but end up stinging the man we love? If we continually shut down our partner when he's vulnerable or is trying to connect, eventually he will stop trying. And who could blame him?

When our fears rise up, we have a choice: stage warfare or open our hearts and bring the truth forward. Think back to the results you've experienced when your fears caused you to retaliate against the man you supposedly loved. Instead of approaching our guy with respect and compassion in order to open up communication, we attack the very person we want to love. A better choice is to become aware of our defense systems and disarm them when they switch on. When we choose to open our hearts and honestly communicate, we invite our partner to do the same. It's not always easy, especially in the heat of the moment, but speaking from the heart always leads to a deeper, more authentic connection.

When Noah and I married, we received a lot of advice, some good and some not. Only one piece of wisdom stuck: "When it gets hard, go deeper." We've practiced this mantra ever since and, as a result, continue to grow ever closer. I use the word *practice* purposely. Although the mantra is short and simple, sometimes the follow-through is damn hard! Honestly, there are moments when I feel I'm under attack or unheard by Noah, and my gremlins move in fast. They want me to rip this man, my beloved, to shreds — not a good tactic if my goal is intimacy! Remembering the words "When it gets hard, go deeper" has been a lifesaver. Not only do I become clearer about the dynamic between my partner and me, but I also realize what is *really* happening in ME. Only then can I sort my fear-based emotions from my heart-centered reality. This man, whose actions have stirred me up, would never hurt me intentionally, although his subconscious fears may try. When our fears are disarmed, we can finally connect.

♥ ME Reflections ♥

Find the truth about how intimate and vulnerable you have been willing to be in your relationships.

- What are your experiences and beliefs regarding intimacy and vulnerability? What would you like to change?
- What makes it hard to be vulnerable with your partner? How do you feel in moments that seem to call for vulnerability? What stops you from being vulnerable and creating intimacy?
- What is your defense mechanism of choice? Do you shut down your partner by stomping on his vulnerability and attacking him? Avoid confrontation by shutting down completely? Acquiesce and then get passive-aggressive? Or maybe something else? How does this damage the intimacy in your relationship?
- Remember a time when you spoke directly from the heart without fear of being hurt. Ask yourself, "What was

special about the person I was with? The situation? The environment?" What do you need to feel safe when vulnerable?

- Are you willing to be intimate with a partner? Emotionally? Spiritually? Physically? If so, what skills do you need to develop? What fears do you need to face? What behaviors do you need to change? And what support do you need, from your partner or from others?

Intimate Connection Requires WE

Developing an intimate relationship takes two people, and both are responsible for being honest and vulnerable. While your guy doesn't have to be perfect, he must be willing and able to own his feelings and share his innermost self. No amount of prodding, harping, or threatening will get your guy to open up if he doesn't have the ability to be vulnerable, the courage to step through his fears, or the maturity to have an honest and open dialogue. And, if he can't or won't have this dialogue, you owe it to yourself to say, "No, I won't settle for a mediocre connection or the business contract. I want more!"

Many of us fall into the trap of taking stereotypes about men and women as the absolute truth. This is especially true for the adage that says men don't talk and women talk too much; men sulk off to their cave, while women try tirelessly to pull them out. Our thoughts create our reality, and when we buy into this bunk, we end up attracting a caveman for a partner and settling for the grunts. The good news is, you don't have to live *your* life according to this stereotype or, for that matter, any other. There is no natural phenomenon that makes all men inexpressive and all women too emotional; not all men push away intimacy, and not all women cling to their partners.

In truth, both men and women want connection and intimacy.

How these bonds manifest differs for all *people*, but not according to gender. We must stop having conversations about why men and women are different from each other and start seeing men and women as *people* first — we're different because we are all individual and unique. When we stop stereotyping our mates, we can actually know them intimately as individuals, not as representatives of their gender.

In my marriage, Noah is the one who won't let the conversation shut down, and I'm the one with the instinct to run off to my cave. Against stereotype, he has the tenderness and patience to draw me out. But I didn't marry a stereotype; I married a person who is unique beyond any limitation our society brands as "the way things are." Each of us has the job of intimately knowing our partner, from his outer persona to his innermost feelings.

❤ ME Reflections ❤

Ask yourself the following questions to gain insight into your guy's (or if you are single, your previous partner's) ability to be vulnerable and intimate.

- Is your guy willing to be vulnerable, to share his innermost feelings? When is he vulnerable and how does he show it? What keeps him from opening up?
- What stereotypes have you branded your partner with? Take another look at him, this time as the human being you love and without the stereotypical characteristics attributed to his gender. Who do you see?
- Do you accept mediocre connection — either physical, emotional, spiritual, or mental — in your relationship? How does your partner contribute to any mediocre connection? How do you contribute? What level of intimacy and connection do you really want?

Intimacy Requires Depth and Curiosity

If asked, "Do you know your partner?" most of us would say, "Yes, of course." And, on some level, this would be true. However, if asked, "Do you know his innermost thoughts, desires, and feelings?" many of us could not answer yes with certainty. How often do we actually listen to our partner, instead of just hearing the words that support our expectations or needs? Intimate partnership requires us to look deeply into the man in our life, way beyond the surface-level connections we often create, and really know him.

Sure, most of us know our guy's pertinent data, and we probably have a decent idea of his goals, likes, dislikes, weaknesses, and strengths. But how close are we to his innermost dreams and fears? How well do we know his true character, not the facade the world sees? And besides knowing *about* it, how often do we *connect* with his soul? How often do we get beyond the demands of daily life, or beyond striving for material achievement, so that our spirits can dance together?

To create intimacy, we must be curious, even passionate, about who our partner is in the depths of his soul. Intimacy demands a deep yearning to touch and connect with the innermost parts of our partner, an intense desire to know *him*. This requires more than talks about our financial future or our common goals — it calls for deeper conversation, daily. Even in the midst of everyday demands, we must make the effort to bond with our mate's spirit, not just with the guy who goes to the office everyday, splits the rent with us, or hangs out playing ball.

A Story about Breaking Conventions to Create Connection

I am blessed that my marriage abounds with intimate connection and meaningful conversation. Noah and I listen intently to each other, speak from our hearts, and engage in real, fulfilling dialogue daily. But truthfully, getting to this point has taken a lot of practice and patience and a continued commitment to intimately knowing ourselves and each other.

This was never more evident than on the day Noah asked me to marry him. I had known the proposal was coming. Two months earlier, while sitting in a coffee shop in San Francisco, we had decided to get married. We'd talked about what marriage meant to each of us, discussed what each wanted from life, and agreed to create an even stronger bond by getting married. After talking about all the important topics a couple should discuss beforehand, we were both excited and really sure about our decision. The only detail to take care of? I asked Noah to pick some future day, unbeknownst to me, to formally ask me to marry him.

So imagine Noah's surprise when he popped the question "Will you marry me?" two months later, on a sunny California beach, and I did not respond, "Yes!" Now, I didn't respond, "No," either. Instead, I felt an urge to do something most bridal books would never recommend: I wanted to stop, not answer the question, and instead create a more intimate connection by taking the conversation deeper. Was I crazy? Ask questions? Have a conversation? Wasn't I just supposed to jump up and down ecstatically and scream, "Yes, of course I will marry you"? That was what I had been conditioned to do, so doing anything else would be plain stupidity, right?

Well, maybe others would think so, but my intuition had ideas of her own! In that moment, she said to me, "You want to know exactly what you're saying yes to, don't you? This moment will affect the rest of your life, so treat it that way." Forming the foundation for my life with this man was foremost on her mind. Taking the conversation deeper was the way to do it. My decision to follow her guidance was one of the best I ever made.

In that moment, I wanted more than what a yes could provide. I wanted intimacy. I had, once before, given the standard "Yes, of course I will marry you!" answer to a man, and that experience had been like being swept into a whirlwind. Although I had felt a flash of connection, the intimacy was soon over, as we jumped onto what I have come to call the "wedding treadmill." It worked like this: Just minutes after I accepted the proposal and we engaged in some snuggling activity, we immediately focused all our energy on everyone *but* the two of us. We started calling people and sharing the good news, and then began the endless, all-consuming wedding planning. Our connection, or lack of it, got lost in all the excitement.

Given a second chance, with Noah, I understood that my commitment to marriage started as soon I said yes. What mattered — for us and our marriage — was the energy created at the start of this new journey. So, taking a deep breath, I said, "Noah, you are my best friend in the whole world and the man I want to share my life with. *And*, I really want to talk about what this means for both of us, right now, in this moment." The conversation I began with him allowed me to connect with my man's soul.

I wasn't sure what Noah's reaction would be, but thankfully, his head didn't start spinning and he didn't turn bright red. He was a little surprised, but he took the time to connect with me at this deeper level, without resistance. If he had refused, I would've known he wasn't my guy. The connection we established in this important moment created the foundation for not only our wedding but, more important, our marriage.

Taking It Deeper

Following are the questions I asked Noah that day on the beach. The intimate foundation they helped create has been invaluable, especially in the moments when my fears about him or the viability of our partnership surfaced. Although I asked these questions at the time of his proposal, they can be asked at any point in a relationship to take the conversation deeper and establish a more authentic bond. Indeed, we've revisited them again and again.

WHAT ARE YOUR INTENTIONS FOR *YOUR* LIFE? This question sheds light on what your guy has planned for *his* life, regardless of your presence in it. You may think you already know the answer, that he wants to be a vice president, a dad, and so on. While such things may be true, intimacy requires more than standard answers like these, which come mostly from the head or a sense of "should." This question addresses a person's soul. Answered authentically, it leads to significant insights into a man and your compatibility as partners.

Asking this question summons a level of seriousness that demands nothing short of honesty. Your mate's response will let you see how together he actually is, regardless of the plans you've made for him. While he doesn't need a five-year plan, he does need to intimately know himself and be willing to share his personal thoughts with you. His answer also provides the opportunity to examine the level of alignment between your personal intentions and his. If you're two people going in different directions, or one moving forward while the other stays put, this is an early sign of a doomed relationship.

If he's nervous or unsure at first, get things started by sharing your intentions. Give the guy a break; this question is intense. If he doesn't have an answer, then you need to ask yourself, "Do I want a mate who hasn't a clue about his life intentions?" Help him move beyond the standard answers and into the depths of his innermost thoughts. If he won't or can't, then your question is "Do I want a partner who can express his life only with his head, not with his heart and soul?"

WHAT ARE YOUR *COMMITMENTS* TO YOURSELF? Although this may sound similar to the previous question, note that intention and commitment are two very different actions. We can intend to do something our whole life and never actually do it. Without commitment, intentions are empty promises. The question prompts the person answering to pause and ask himself, "What do I really commit to? What promises am I willing to make to myself?" It's a big question by any standard, since stating our commitments requires us to have the integrity to honor our word. His reply basically says, "I make these commitments to myself. You can count on them." Putting this stake in the ground can help you avoid a relationship full of disappointment. Before a person commits to WE, it's critical for him or her to commit to ME. When people make commitments to themselves, rather than to someone else, their chances of following through are much better. And you're more likely to be honest with yourself about who your guy really is.

Because I was committed to a life of personal exploration, I believed my partner had to be committed to his own growth. Although I knew that Noah *wanted* to be the best Noah possible, we both needed his commitment as we entered into marriage. In the moments since, when I have been scared that he was going to stop growing, I remember his commitment, and relax. And, in his own time, he always moves ahead. This promise has been invaluable to the health and sustainability of our relationship.

WHAT DOES THE COMMITMENT WE'RE MAKING TO EACH OTHER (THAT IS, MARRIAGE, MOVING IN TOGETHER, AND SO ON) MEAN TO YOU? HOW IS THIS DIFFERENT FROM WHAT WE HAVE NOW? This question helps ferret out how much your guy has thought about this new level of your relationship, and it sheds light on what it means to him. Is this next step something he's taking just because it's the next logical step in the progression of life? Or are his heart and soul really engaged in this next adventure with you? Marriage, living together, or otherwise making a long-term commitment is a choice, not something you do because everyone else is doing it.

What do you want to motivate your partner as he enters into this commitment: obligation and societal pressure, or a knowing in his soul? Is it okay for him to be on autopilot, or do you prefer him to be fully aware and present?

This question also reveals your guy's expectations about the type of commitment you are each making. Every person experiences a relationship and marriage differently, and therefore each has unique expectations. You may have already talked about choices such as children, finances, jobs, security, and so on, but this question is different. It's not about the contract; it's about the deep assumptions we have about a partner when it comes to the type of commitment we're making. Exploring this question together will tell you what you each expect from yourselves and the relationship.

These questions were not some torturous exercise I devised to make my partner uncomfortable or to give myself a false sense of security. They cleared away assumptions, set up expectations, and allowed us to see each other's truest self, providing a strong foundation for our relationship as we moved on to new terrain. If you choose to take it deeper with your partner, listen carefully to his answers. Be fully present, hear every word, and see your partner for the unique individual he is. Remember your intuition; be acutely aware of what she sees, hears, and otherwise senses. Take her feelings as truth. Don't settle for one- or two-word answers from your partner. Know that you have a right to an intimate connection with him. Taking it deeper is a required part of choosing ME before WE. Are you willing to do it?

❤ ME Reflections ❤

Think about knowing your partner much more intimately than you do today by answering the following questions.

- What do you yearn to know about your guy, far below the surface, deep in his soul? What makes you curious about *this* man?
- If you look at his unique self, separate from you, what do you see? How would seeing him, without your projections or influence, strengthen your connection?
- If you want to know more, how can you invite him to set his innermost self out in the open?
- Remembering your Core Four, what questions will help you be certain that who your guy really is matches what you desire in a partner?
- What concerns you most about this man and your relationship? How might taking it deeper help? How can you connect with him regarding your concerns?

Then turn the focus on yourself and answer the three questions from the chapter.

- What are your intentions for *your* life?
- What are your commitments to yourself?
- What does the commitment you are making to each other now (that is, marriage, moving in together, and so on) mean to you? How is this different from what you have now?

And then think about what you expect from your partner's responses.

- How do you want your partner to answer? What words do you want to hear?
- What are you most afraid he will say? Not say?

Like everything else we've talked about, it all starts with you. How intimately the two of you connect depends on your willingness and ability to be vulnerable and honest. You deserve the love, respect, and joy that comes from deep, intimate partnership, but you have to make a commitment to yourself first.

I have one last choice to ask you to make, and it's as critical in your journey to choose ME before WE as the other choices and promises you've already made, to know, love, trust, honor, and be honest with ME. Even if we stay single for the rest of our lives, we all need connection with others. It's one of the most priceless gifts of being alive. So *choose* the quality of the connections you want to have by making promises to yourself now.

Use the following vows as a guide to finding the promises you want to make to yourself, the commitments that will ensure that in your relationships you always put the most important partner first — you.

◎ MY VOWS FOR CONNECTION ◎

- In my intimate partnerships with men, I promise myself...
- In my intimate relationships with the people I love, I promise myself...
- In an effort to be vulnerable and honest in all of my relationships, I promise myself...

A Final Note

*C*hoosing ME is something that any woman can decide to do for the rest of her life. By doing so, we get to know ourselves better, love ourselves more, and allow ourselves to experience the kind of happiness that sticks. Every woman, including you, is a magnificent, beautiful spirit who deserves to be completely in love with herself, with or without a man. From this place of completeness, we can empower ourselves to choose a partner who truly honors our soul. We owe ourselves this possibility. No one else can make the choice for us. And, as we do this for ourselves, so we support every other woman and girl in doing the same.

My hope is that you leave this book with more than you arrived with, in the form of possibilities and a commitment to yourself. My wish is that, as you continue on your own path, you will fall in love with yourself, again and again, for the rest of your life.

— *Christine Arylo*

Inspiration, Ideas, and More

I found words of wisdom in the following books, songs, and poems that I discovered along my path. You may find them helpful too, while uncovering new possibilities and a deeper understanding on your journey to fall madly in love with your unique and brilliant self. Enjoy the discovery!

A Healthy You

The Female Power Within: A Guide to Living a Gentler, More Meaningful Life, by Marilyn Graman and Maureen Walsh

The Power of Now: A Guide to Spiritual Enlightenment, by Eckhart Tolle

A New Earth: Awakening to Your Life's Purpose, by Eckhart Tolle

The Places That Scare You: A Guide to Fearlessness in Difficult Times, by Pema Chödrön

Lie- and Illusion-Shattering

The Way to Love: The Last Meditations of Anthony de Mello, by Anthony de Mello

Codependent No More: How to Stop Controlling Others and Start Caring for Yourself, by Melody Beattie

Awareness: The Perils and Opportunities of Reality, by Anthony de Mello

Abundance and Manifesting

Creating Money: Attracting Abundance, by Sanaya Roman and Duane Packer

The Power of Intention: Learning to Co-create Your World Your Way, by Wayne Dyer

The Dynamic Laws of Prosperity, by Catherine Ponder

The Soul of Money: Transforming Your Relationship with Money and Life, by Lynne Twist

Loving ME

The Art of Happiness: A Handbook for Living, by His Holiness the Dalai Lama and Howard C. Cutler, MD

Acoustic Soul, by India Arie (CD)

Testimony: Volume 1, Life & Relationship, by India Arie (CD)

Choosing Your Copilot

*The Wisdom of the Enneagram: The Complete Guide to Psychological and Spiritual Growth for the Nine Personality Type*s, by Don Richard Riso and Russ Hudson

Intuition

Developing Intuition: Practical Guidance for Daily Life, by Shakti Gawain

Divine Intuition: Your Guide to Creating a Life You Love, by Lynn A. Robinson

WE

Soul Mates: Honoring the Mysteries of Love and Relationship, by Thomas Moore

Intimacy

The Invitation, by Oriah Mountain Dreamer

The Dance of Intimacy: A Woman's Guide to Courageous Acts of Change in Key Relationships, by Harriet Lerner

Choosing ME before WE

Book Club Chat

FIND THE LOVE YOU WANT WITH YOUR
GIRLFRIENDS BY YOUR SIDE!

As a formal book club or an informal gathering, do the *Choosing ME before WE* Book Club Chat together and you'll find yourself nodding your head, laughing, and creating a closer bond with the women you love, including you!

How to Throw a Great Book Club Chat
Because there is so much great conversation to dive into, I recommend choosing a few chapters or one of the three parts (ME, HE, or WE) as your focus for your book club chat. You can also hold multiple gatherings with your girlfriends, choosing a section each time you meet. Prior to your gathering, ask women to think about the questions and bring their reactions and insights to create a real, wise, and fun girlfriend conversation.

ME

ONE: Knowing ME
What are the dreams I have for my life?
Start a list of your 108 life dreams and share them. If you don't know your dreams, you can't expect a partner to support them. (108 is the most significant number in the universe. Google it!)

TWO: Truthfully ME
What lie am I telling myself about me or my relationship?
Then take it deeper by answering these questions: 1. What's the cost of this lie? 2. What's the benefit? 3. What's the truth? 4. What's the consequence of the truth? 5. What action will I take to address the truth?

THREE: Loving ME
What do I really love about ME? What is hard for me to love about ME?
Make a list of all the things you love about yourself (and commit to getting it to 108!). Make a list of things that are hard for you to love (and make sure this list is much shorter). Ask your girlfriends for ideas on how you can learn to love those hard-to-love spots more.

FOUR: Trusting ME

When have I listened to my intuition and won? When have I listened to my Inner Mean Girl and lost?

Share a story about a time you acted from intuition and made great relationship choices. Share a story in which you didn't, and compare the results.

FIVE: Honoring ME

Where am I settling in my life — tolerating or procrastinating? What do I really desire?

Get real about what you are settling for and take a stand for giving your heart and soul what they crave. If you dare, take this vow together as a group: "I will never settle for less than my heart and soul desire." Powerful girlfriend pact! And then support each other to keep that vow.

HE

SIX: Choosing Your Core Four

What are my Core Four, and how can I make them even more powerful?

Share your Core Four with each other in an effort to make sure your Core Four is as strong and heart-centered as possible. Heartstorm, share, and inspire each other to choose words that carry energy magnetic and powerful enough to call in your best partner!

WE

SEVEN: Getting Wise About WE

What can I shift inside me to create more trust, respect, intimacy, and unconditional love in my relationships?

Take a look inside and notice how and when you push any of these four aspects of true partnership out of your life — in all your relationships, including those with romantic partners, relatives, and friends. What's hard for you about trust, respect, intimacy, and unconditional love? What's easy? And what does each one really mean to you?

EIGHT: Getting the Intimacy We Crave

How open am I to receiving and giving love?

What's your love quotient? This is your ability to let love in from another freely and also to give love out fully. Most of us have stunted love quotients in need of expanding! Describe your relationship to both vulnerability and physical affection and ask your girlfriends to rate your love quotient on both receiving and giving love.

Visit www.mebeforewe.com for more fabulous and free LOVE resources!

♥

About the Author

$\mathcal{A}$fter earning her MBA from Northwestern University's Kellogg School of Management and spending over twelve years marketing big brands such as Gap Inc., Visa, and Frito-Lay, Christine Arylo traded in building images for corporations for a chance to inspire women to break free from their limiting self-images. Merging her professional experience and extensive leadership and coaching training with her spiritual journey, Christine now works with women and girls as a catalyst for change. Christine's clients include entrepreneurs, executives, and people seeking a personal path. As an author, speaker, and transformational teacher, Christine leads powerful virtual and in-person experiences for women around the world. Her opinions have been featured on ABC, CBS, FOX, and E! Entertainment TV. Known as the Queen of Self-Love, Christine created Madly in Love with ME™, an international day of self-love on February 13th, and she cofounded Inner Mean Girl Reform School™, a virtual school dedicated to transforming women's self-sabotaging voices. Christine lives in the San Francisco Bay Area with her soul partner, Noah, and their Siberian husky.

Inner Mean Girl
REFORM SCHOOL
Where Women Come to Transform Inner Critics Into Inner Superheroines

Inner Mean Girl Reform School offers online classes, home study programs, workshops, and 40-day self-love practices that give women the tools and experiences they need to transform their self-sabotaging patterns and beliefs into new self-empowering habits. Thousands of women on every continent have taken a stand by saying NO! to being so darn hard on themselves. For more information, visit www.innermeangirl.com. And stop by and join the Inner Mean Girl Revolution on our Facebook Fan Page.

Madly in Love with ME™ is an international self-love movement dedicated to making self-love a tangible reality for women and girls around the world. Launching every year on February 13th, the official day of self-love, Madly in Love with ME offers self-love inspiration in many forms, including a free Madly in Love with ME Guidebook and an official ME-heart token necklace. www.madlyinlovewithme.com.

Step Up Women's Network is a national nonprofit dedicated to strengthening community resources for women and girls. It offers teen empowerment programs, women's health education and advocacy support, and professional mentorship opportunities designed to help women and girls feel great about themselves. Because I believe in the power of what they do, a percentage of my proceeds from this book will go to Step Up Women's Network. Check out their website at www.suwn.org.

NEW WORLD LIBRARY is dedicated to publishing books and other media that inspire and challenge us to improve the quality of our lives and the world.

We are a socially and environmentally aware company, and we strive to embody the ideals presented in our publications. We recognize that we have an ethical responsibility to our customers, our staff members, and our planet.

We serve our customers by creating the finest publications possible on personal growth, creativity, spirituality, wellness, and other areas of emerging importance. We serve New World Library employees with generous benefits, significant profit sharing, and constant encouragement to pursue their most expansive dreams.

As a member of the Green Press Initiative, we print an increasing number of books with soy-based ink on 100 percent postconsumer-waste recycled paper. Also, we power our offices with solar energy and contribute to nonprofit organizations working to make the world a better place for us all.

Our products are available
in bookstores everywhere.
For our catalog, please contact:

New World Library
14 Pamaron Way
Novato, California 94949

Phone: 415-884-2100 or 800-972-6657
Catalog requests: Ext. 50
Orders: Ext. 52
Fax: 415-884-2199
Email: escort@newworldlibrary.com

To subscribe to our electronic newsletter, visit
www.newworldlibrary.com